THE TWO-CAREER FAMILY

THE TWO-CAREER FAMILY

Lynda Lytle Holmstrom

SCHENKMAN PUBLISHING COMPANY

Cambridge, Massachusetts

Distributed by General Learning Press

Schenkman books are distributed by

General Learning Press
250 James Street
Morristown, New Jersey 07960

Library of Congress Catalog Card Number: 70-189095
Copyright © 1972 Lynda Lytle Holmstrom
All rights reserved.
Schenkman Publishing Company
Cambridge, Massachusetts 02138

This book is set in Linotype Palatino
Printed in the United States of America

Contents

ACKNOWLEDGMENTS

This book is the result of the efforts of many people. Above all, I wish to thank Everett Cherrington Hughes, Philip E. Slater, and Irving Kenneth Zola for both intellectual stimulation and the encouragement that they provided throughout the study. Without their interest, it is doubtful whether the book ever would have been completed. It is impossible to list all of the people with whom I discussed aspects of the research. However, I should like to also mention Rose Laub Coser, F. Ross Holmstrom, and Jane Gaudette Jones, since discussions with them were especially helpful. I also wish to thank Robert S. Weiss, who provided advice on the analysis of qualitative data.

I am indebted to the men and women who took time out of their busy schedules to be interviewed. Without their cooperation, there would have been no study.

Many thanks are due Sheila Segal for her editorial help and suggestions. A special acknowledgment also is due Sandra Reitman for her careful and efficient typing of the final manuscript. Typing in the early stages of the project was done by Dimitra Macris, Selma Mazer, and Betty Griffin.

The research upon which this book is based was funded primarily by a grant, No. 91-23-68-45, from the Manpower Administration of the U. S. Department of Labor. Boston College provided funds for the preparation of the manuscript. The interpretations and conclusions presented are of course my own. They do not necessarily represent the official position or policy of the Department of Labor, nor should any of the other people to whom I am indebted be held responsible for them.

Additionally, I want to thank the following authors and publishers who permitted me to quote from their works:

Philip E. Slater, "Some Social Consequences of Temporary Systems", in *The Temporary Society*, by Warren G. Bennis and Philip E. Slater (New York: Harper and Row, 1968). Copyright © 1968 by Warren G. Bennis and Philip E. Slater.

Everett C. Hughes, "Neo-Feminism: An Essay on Woman's Work" (Mimeographed).

William J. Goode, *The Family* (Englewood Cliffs, New Jersey: Prentice-Hall, 1964). Copyright © 1964 by Prentice-Hall, Inc.

To ROSS

1

One Home, Two Careers

Our society makes it very difficult to have two careers in the same family. It simply is assumed that in a middle-class couple only one spouse will have a serious profession. It is the husband who typically has the demanding occupational role. The wife has either no occupation or one that is subordinate in importance to that of her husband.

What happens when both a husband and wife do have highly demanding careers? What are the resulting career patterns and problems? These are questions that are gaining in importance today. It is obvious that the long-term trend is to have more and more women in the labor force. Not only do single women work, but wives and mothers are working in increasing numbers. Furthermore, we are now witnessing the second wave of the women's movement. There is an increasing demand for opportunities for women and a decline in their willingness to always take second place. Thus it seems more important than ever before to know what happens when wives embark on careers.

To investigate this question, a detailed study was done of a group of couples in which both the husband and wife were professionals, the wife having an independent career of her own. Although it appears that the two-career family will become more common in the future, it is now the exception rather than the rule. These couples are therefore "bucking the system," and they have had to face a whole series of barriers which assume that only one spouse will work and that, furthermore, it is the husband who will do so.

Many of the barriers encountered by these people fall into three main categories — the rigid structure of the professions, the isolation of the small modern family, and the current equation of masculinity with superiority. They include such things as the definition of career as requiring single-minded devotion to work, frequent pressures to move geographically for career advancement, the expectation that some jobs will be held by men while their wives devote time and energy to ancillary activities such as entertaining, and the difficulty

1

of raising children when both spouses work. Although these barriers may be altered or removed in the future, at present they constitute severe obstacles for the two-career family.

One major obstacle to two careers in the family arises from conventional expectations of how a career, in the strictest sense, is to be pursued. One usually is expected to be single-minded about pursuing a career and to subordinate the rest of one's activities to it. Sanctions are applied against those who are unwilling or unable to do this. Many employers will not employ a person for less than full time; or if they do, they do not consider the person a full member of the organization. Schools are often unwilling to accept a person for professional training unless he or she attends full time, and a history of interrupted work or study activity is often a significant disadvantage. In addition to all these pressures, the expectation is that the activities of other family members will be subordinated to those of the person pursuing a profession. Thus, with the prevalence of these patterns and perceptions in a society, it is extremely difficult to have two fully developed careers in the same family.

The occupational pressures that exist for people to move about often constitute another barrier to the two-career family. These pressures affect the lives of people in occupations as disparate as the military and the academic. In many cases career advancement is more rapid if one can move about or stay put without having to consider the interests of other family members. Above all, it is an advantage to be mobile, for this gives one access to more job opportunities. In many professions there are incentives to shift from employer to employer rather than going up the ladder in a single institution. A change of employer often means a change of city too. Furthermore, many employers themselves move people about. The "corporation transfer" is probably one of the most frequently discussed examples. In short, mobility is an expected part of business and professional life today. If one wants to stay with the company, then one goes across the continent at the organization's beck and call. But the converse is also important, for it is also an advantage to be able to stay in a given place as long as necessary in order to honor the commitments that one makes or attain the advancement that one desires.

Thus the system favors the person who can decide when and where to move with the assurance that the other members of the family will follow along automatically. Clearly these expectations impose a hardship on both partners in a two-career family. It would be to each partner's advantage to be the one to decide where to live. They face a dilemma. Career opportunities may tempt them to go off in different directions, yet to do so means sacrificing at least part of their life together.

There is an expectation that for certain jobs two people will be available to fulfill the duties associated with one job. The position itself will be held by the husband. The wife will be available to perform the auxiliary activities which are connected with it. Most often she is expected to entertain. The president — of the country, the corporation, or the university — is expected to have a wife to act as hostess. The pattern is most visible when one looks at the lives of such men in high places. But it occurs at other levels of government, business, and academia as well. This too is a barrier to the two-career family. A wife who takes on such duties has far less time and energy left to follow a demanding career of her own.

These are only a few of the occupational barriers facing the two-career family. They, and many others, will be discussed later in detail.[1] Many are simply characteristics of occupations which have been elaborated to the point of rigidity for its own sake. In other words, they are conditions of employment which are retained blindly as a matter of principle, rather than as a result of any rational evaluation about whether they are actually necessary for getting the work done. Must a career demand a full-time schedule, an itinerant life for rapid advancement, professional entertaining, and so on? Perhaps people could work effectively some other way — employed part time, living in the same place, having fewer work-related social gatherings — but, at present, anyone who wants to work in such an unorthodox manner must fight for the privilege.

The isolation of the small modern family also is a barrier to having two professions. This is because of the enormous difficulties that this isolation causes for child rearing. In the typical middle-class family, the husband and wife, with their children, live by themselves apart from other relatives. Thus they must be self-sufficient in many ways which would not be necessary if other relatives were nearby. The isolation is especially apparent on a day-to-day basis. Obviously, relatives still see each other, visit, and exchange help, even if they live at a great distance. But this is hard to do in a routine manner. A woman, for example, may travel to help her daughter for a week or so when a grandchild is born, but soon she must return to her own home. Furthermore, other possible substitutes such as servants and child-care centers generally are not available. Thus, child rearing, a task which in previous times was shared with other people, now falls solely on the parents. Since most men leave home each day to hold a job, this task falls mainly on the wife, who remains at home to care for the children when they are small. This aspect of the family, as well as other characteristics, will be discussed more later. It will become apparent that at present, the family, like occupations, is set up in ways which assume that only one marriage partner will have a career.[2]

Structurally, it would not make much difference which marital partner had the career. In other words, if the roles of the sexes were simply reversed — with the women working and the men staying home — many of the institutional arrangements could remain the same. One would simply get a mirror image of the present system: the husband would be able to follow the wife on her itinerant circuit of jobs and the husband would be able to remain at home and take care of the children. In this sense, the issue is not who has the career. Rather, the issue is that having two careers in one married couple constitutes a major structural difficulty.

Attitudinally, however, it does make a great deal of difference which marital partner follows a profession. Attitudinally, a salient feature of the occupational world and the family — indeed of the whole society — is the belief now held that male supremacy is legitimate and justified. Masculinity is equated with superiority, femininity is equated with inferiority. This attitude is held not only by many men, but also by many women. Thus it is the men who are expected to engage in those activities which the society defines as more prestigious, as having higher status, as contributing more to society, as more exciting, as more challenging. If both sexes engage in the same activity, the men are supposed to be better at it than the women. Within any given family, it is typically the husband who has the career, or, if both work, he has the "more serious" career. Thus one cannot discuss the two-career family without also discussing the issue of male supremacy and women's rights.

This recognition that our society now equates masculinity with superiority leads one to a parting of the ways with another sociological school of thought. This other school of thought proclaims the necessity of a sex-linked division of labor. It insists that in order to prevent competition between a husband and wife, they must be kept from engaging in the same activities. For these theorists, the central issue to look at is the amount of similarity or dissimilarity in the activities of the spouses, and since these theorists see that a husband and a wife in our society usually do different things, they simply conclude that competition has been prevented. They assume that the problem is solved and that now the sexes are not engaged "in a race." In contrast, this present analysis suggests that the sexes *are* engaged

in a race — and that, according to the current rules, the man is supposed to win. Thus the main issue to look at is not whether the husband and wife do the same activities. Rather the issue to focus on is
the present cultural norm which states that the husband should be
superior to his wife in any way that is important to him.

It is crucial to recognize that all these structural and attitudinal barriers exist. It is frequently alleged that all opportunities are open to
women — even married women — and that they just have not taken
advantage of them. However, the present study suggests that it is
not surprising that there are so few two-career families; the surprising thing is that any such families exist at all.

The two-career couples who were studied organized their lives in
ways to combat many of the barriers mentioned above. This will be
seen throughout the book. In reading about the life styles that they
fashioned, two factors are important to keep in mind, both associated
with swimming against the tide. One factor is that these couples had
to develop their own *individual* solutions as they went along; they
had to invent their own *ad hoc* arrangements, for our society really
offers no *institutionalized* solutions to the problems that the two-career
family faces. There are no pre-existing patterns or models; therefore,
innovation and persistence are essential. For example, most graduate
schools are still reluctant to take part-time students on an equal standing with regular students. Thus, if a couple feels that part-time at-
tendance would solve certain problems of two careers for them, they
have to fight for the privilege and sell the school on the idea. Furthermore, our society really offers no *collective* solutions, such as group
child care, to the problems faced by the two-career family. Each
couple is left to their own devices, rather than having any sharing of
responsibility. Because little exists in the way of group day-care for
children, each couple must make their own arrangements. The experiences of the couples in the study suggest some such solutions which
might be developed, and they are presented in the concluding chapter.

A second factor to keep in mind is that often difficulties are connected with the *newness* of a social pattern rather than being inherent
in that pattern. The two-career family does represent a relatively new
life style in the contemporary United States, and thus one would
expect many problems that these people face to be due to, or at least
compounded by, the fact that the social pattern is new and atypical.[3]
This point would hold at several levels, including those of coping
with internalized psychological conflict, facing outside criticism, and
making practical arrangements. To take one example, if the parents
both work when their child is young, then some changes must be

made in the method of child rearing. This may lead the parents — and especially the mother — to experience feelings of guilt about supposedly neglecting the child, just because they are not following the typical methods of child rearing. They also may be subjected to the criticism from outsiders — from relatives, neighbors, and the school guidance counsellor. On top of this, they will have to cope with the practical difficulties of setting up child-care arrangements.

Thus the traditional family structure, like the inflexible occupational structure, perpetuates the assumption that there will be only one career per married couple. One spouse — presumably the husband — is to engage in the single-minded pursuit of career goals. The woman is to spend her days in domestic activities, and the wife and children are to serve the man's needs. They are to adapt their schedule to his, to move when necessary, entertain for him, and so on. They are not supposed to have interests which might conflict with his. It is in this sense, that two-career families are "going against the system." There are indeed special problems associated with going against the system, and, while it may be true that people do not adapt automatically or easily to new social patterns, this does not necessarily mean that the new patterns should not be tried.

NOTES

1. It is merely for the sake of brevity that the terms "family" and "occupation" are often used without qualification. To be precise, this discussion of the family deals with features found especially in the white, non-rural, middle-class or upper-middle-class family. The discussion of occupations deals with features found especially at the professional and managerial level.

2. Most of the analysis in the book would also hold for two-career couples who were not legally married. Many of the same career problems would occur for a man and woman who considered themselves a couple even though not married. Anti-nepotism rules would be one of the few exceptions to this.

3. Rossi, writing in 1964 and using research on intermarriage as an example, has discussed the reluctance of sociologists to recognize that certain failures may be due to the newness of a social pattern. Alice S. Rossi, "Equality Between the Sexes: An Immodest Proposal," Daedalus, 93 (Spring, 1964), p. 612.

To Understand the Two-Career Family

DECIDING WHO TO STUDY

The problem before us was to find out what it was like to be in a two-career family. There are many combinations of professions that result in such a family. One thinks of doctors married to physicists, doctors married to doctors, classicists married to businessmen, nurses married to lawyers, and so on. The number of occupations, and more importantly the number of their possible combinations in a marriage, seems endless. One cannot look at all these people simultaneously; one simply could not make sense of a study which attempted to include all of these at once. Thus the sensible thing to do is to choose some particular group to study.

The question a researcher asks is "what group of people can I study whose experiences will highlight the issues that I am trying to understand"? The rule for selecting a group is to choose one that will give you insight into the problem. With this aim in mind, it was decided to look at couples where the women had professions in the humanities and sciences. These occupations illustrate very nicely problems that occur in numerous occupations in our society today — the kinds of issues, for example, that were discussed in the introductory chapter. Obviously, people in these fields have some problems which are unique to them, but many problems they face are common to careers in other fields of endeavor — whether they be in the business world or in radical politics. It was the problems that this group shared with others that were emphasized in the study.

Another important decision that was made was to keep the study small in size. Large surveys have already been done on female participation in the labor force. The present study was made to complement these existing surveys by probing the story behind the numerical trends to get at many subtleties which are difficult to capture on punched IBM cards. For this reason, only twenty couples with two careers were interviewed.

Once the broad outlines of the study were decided, it was necessary to pick specific couples. Couples were chosen according to five characteristics:

The first characteristic was the wife's occupation, as already indicated. The women selected had professions in the humanities, social sciences, or the physical and life sciences. These occupations were chosen because they illustrate several things common to many occupations in our society today. Like most occupations, these offer little opportunity for free-lance work; instead one needs an affiliation with an institution — university, business, hospital — to carry out the work, and these institutions frequently have rules against the employment of couples. In these occupations, like many, there often is pressure to move about from employer to employer — often to another city — in order to advance one's career. Further, these are professions for which a long educational and training period is required. (Incidentally, the term "profession" is used rather loosely throughout the book and includes many groups that a strict definition of the term might exclude; for example, scientists who do not have clients, and people who work within a bureaucracy.)

The second characteristic was marriage. Only married people were studied. The reason for this is obvious. Since a main focus was to be on the strains between the world of work and the family, it made more sense to study people who were in families rather than single.

The third characteristic was age. Most of the women selected were between the ages of thirty-five and forty-five; the rest were somewhat older. A deliberate decision was made not to take any woman under the age of thirty-five, for the aim was to find out what couples actually did when faced with the problems of two careers. To find this out you have to wait until people have had certain concrete experiences and made certain concrete decisions. You have to wait until people have had several jobs or job offers, until they have faced the issue of moving, until they actually have children or make the final decision never to have them. It is not as meaningful to ask about these things in the abstract. It is all too easy to say the wife should have equal opportunity, but the real question is what happens when it comes down to brass tacks. What happens when the wife receives a much better offer in another city and the husband does not want to move? What happens when the baby sitter suddenly cannot come and both partners have important appointments at work? For this information you have to wait until people have had the experience and then ask them what they did — not what they think they would do. A few preliminary interviews with younger couples showed that this kind of information could not be gathered from them in as meaningful a way.

The fourth characteristic was locale. The couples were all within the Greater Boston and Amherst areas, mainly the Boston area. The disadvantages of limiting the locale were minimal. There seemed to be little danger of getting only a Bostonian point of view given the high rate of mobility in our society. It was assumed that many couples would have lived much of their lives in other areas. This turned out to be true. Many people had moved numerous times, and of all the people interviewed, only one person was 100% local — born, raised, educated, and employed strictly within Greater Boston. The advantages of limiting the locale were considerable. It seemed desirable to select couples in areas where many job opportunities were available. Boston has a great concentration and variety of employing institutions. Amherst also has numerous employers. Moreover, there was no unemployment problem at the time of the interviews. This meant that the study could concentrate on looking at issues other than the availability of jobs which affect whether and how a married woman practices her profession.

The fifth characteristic was the career experience of the wife. Women were chosen who had pursued careers. They had completed their professional education — for this group that meant obtaining the doctorate — and they were employed in professional positions at the time of the interview.

The main focus was to be on the two-career couples. However, a kind of blindness can occur if a researcher looks at only one type of case. Since an understanding of the two-career family depends on seeing how it departs from a one-career family, it was decided to also interview a small number of couples in which the wife curtailed her career. Seven such couples were interviewed for comparison. This information was used to make visible certain findings that otherwise would have been overlooked.

These comparison couples were chosen in the same way as the other couples except for the career experience of the wife. The first four characteristics—occupational field, marriage, age, locale—were the same. Only the fifth characteristic, career experience of the wife, was different. The women chosen for comparison had significantly limited their careers. Most were women who had had professional training but were unemployed. They held an advanced degree such as a master's or doctorate, but when interviewed they had been out of the labor force for a long time. They had been away from their fields anywhere from seven to twelve years. A few were women who, after several years interruption, had returned to work part time but had never completed the graduate education program that they had started.

An understanding of the two-career family depends on seeing how it differs from the more typical family. Throughout the book, the situation of the two-career family — the "professional" couples — is presented first. Then the comparative situation of the one-career family — the "traditional" couples — is sketched in order to make the differences between them more apparent.

The choice of these labels "professional" and "traditional" requires a word of explanation. It was very difficult to pick terms for referring to these two types of couples. On the one hand, a long accurate description such as "couples with career-relinquishing wives" is too tedious. On the other hand, any short adjective has value-laden connotations. "Professional" and "traditional" finally were chosen because they seemed more neutral than other alternatives. Even so, they cause some problems. For example, professional often implies prestige. And in our future-oriented society, labelling something as traditional may have unfavorable connotations. But it must be emphasized that these terms were not chosen to reflect value judgments. They are not meant to imply that one life style is better than the other. The dilemma is simply that one must use identifying words, and these seem less bothersome than others.

Readers who want to know in detail about the logic of the study should consult the appendix. There, the methodological questions that sociologists worry about — generalizability, criteria for judging whether a sample is adequate, the relative merits of different types of studies — are discussed at some length. For the general reader, the discussion here probably will suffice.

HOW THE INFORMATION WAS OBTAINED

Obviously, no list of two-career families existed. So names of people to be interviewed were obtained through a variety of informal means — professional directories and associations, college catalogues, newspaper articles, and referrals by professional people. Because the wives of most men do not have careers, it was decided to search for names the other way around — to find wives with careers, assuming that their husbands would also. This assumption held up.

Information was obtained by interviewing people in their homes or places of work. Husbands and wives were interviewed separately.

The interviews were very flexible in style, guided only by a general list of topics to be discussed. This made it possible to also discuss issues that the people themselves brought up. In this way issues came to light which had not been thought of when planning the study. The information obtained in interviews was supplemented by information from a variety of other souces. Biographical directories, observations of the home, family, or office made during the interview, and book reviews of their published works were used this way. But the words of the husbands and wives themselves are the primary source of the observations and conclusions suggested in this study.

3

The Life Cycle of the Family

> *I always thought that I would get married, but it wasn't the goal.*
> Professional wife

> *Marriage for me had priority. The best thing was to get married and then think about professional life later.*
> Traditional wife

Our present society has many expectations regarding family life. For one thing, the life cycle of the family is to follow a certain timetable. Not only are you to marry, but you are to do so by a given age. Not only are you to have children, but you are to have them by a given age. Our society gives more latitude in these matters than many other societies do. But, even so, eyebrows are raised if the wife is still childless by her late twenties, and certainly if she is over thirty! And if no children are born, people will keep asking why.

Families are also expected to have a certain structure. We expect today that the household will consist of father, mother, and their children, but no other relatives, and we presume the couple will follow a division of labor in which each sex is assigned its special tasks.

All these current expectations have behind them the assumption that there will be only one career in the family. Our ideas about the life cycle make it difficult to launch two careers while still marrying and having children "on time." Our type of family structure — especially its isolation and its division of labor, discussed in a later chapter — makes it difficult for both spouses to work while raising children.

The two-career family thus goes counter to the family customs that now prevail. It therefore would not be surprising to find a different life cycle in such cases. That is what this chapter is about.

THE DOUBLE BIND

Our present family customs leave professional women in a double bind. No matter which alternative they choose, they lose. On the one hand, if they marry they step into the role of wife. This role as presently defined is incompatible with the full pursuit of one's own career. On the other hand, if they remain single, they face the stigma of spinsterhood. People, as they become adults, are expected to found families of their own. They are not expected — indeed hardly permitted — to go through life as single, unattached individuals, lacking spouse and children. These pressures toward marriage and parenthood are especially forceful for women. The stereotypes abound that a woman cannot develop her humanity to the fullest extent without fusion with a male personality, that the female personality by nature is destined to domestic pursuits, and that a woman must fulfill herself as a person through marriage and motherhood.[1]

The labels attached to the unmarried woman, unless in a convent, have been derogatory. The unmarried girl soon becomes the spinster, and the spinster the old maid. The woman deliberately may have turned down marriage, but she will be criticized by others who say that she is shirking her responsibilties as a woman or that marriage has passed her by. "No positive values whatever are attached to spinsterhood within the accepted framework of roles. The spinster is regarded as having failed in the essential effort of women: to find a husband and raise a family."[2] The stigma of being unmarried may be removed in the future, but it is still with us today.

Not only single women, but occupationally successful women in general find their claims to recognition limited by the sacred values attached to the housewife role.[3] The only way out of the impasse may be to try to do everything. This is the "superwoman" solution in which career, wife, and mother roles are all combined. The trouble is that this solution is seldom practicable.

This indeed leaves women in a double bind. If they remain single and opt solely for careers, they will be accused of having failed as women. If they try through marriage and motherhood to succeed "as women," they impose severe occupational handicaps on themselves.

MARRIAGE

When They Married and How They Viewed It
In view of this double bind, it is interesting to note that the marriage

rate among certain groups of career women is often quite low. Female business executives often do not marry. In a recent study of women with successful careers in business, half married and half did not. And, incidentally, even those who did marry remained single until at least age thirty-five.[4] The marriage rate among female doctorates has been similar. Women who received doctorates in 1957-58 were studied several years later when many were in their forties, and even by then only fifty-five per cent had married.[5] This rate of marriage is low, both in comparison to males with similar education and occupations and in comparison to women in the general population.

The attitudes of the professional women interviewed in the present study reveal that they were less oriented toward marriage than most women are. All twenty were married, since this was one of the characteristics by which they were chosen. But it is clear — both in attitude and deed — that an early marriage was not their sole preoccupation. This is not surprising in view of the low marriage rates described above and the difficulties of combining marriage and career.

Although most of these twenty professional women did marry while in their twenties, four "married late." These four married for the first time when they were thirty years or older. Furthermore, slightly over one third were thirty years or older when they married their present husband.

As to attitude, a third of the professional women either expressed some reservation over getting married or they explained that marriage was not *the* goal. They said that they had not seen themselves as getting married. They were very ambivalent about taking the step of marriage. They turned down some men who were opposed to careers for women. They had especially long courtships because of apprehension about how two careers would mesh. Or they did not see marriage as the first priority. One woman explained:

> *I always thought that I would get married, but it wasn't the goal. I took it as a very natural thing that eventually I would meet the right person. . . . At that time, being young and foolish, I saw no difficulty whatsoever in attempting to combine (laughter) marriage and career. . . . I wasn't going to go out and look for a man or worry if a man didn't appear, if the right man didn't appear, because I had the feeling that there would be somebody appearing who would agree that I should go on and do my graduate work, or, if I had finished it, that I should go on and pursue my own interests.*[6]

Another woman explained that there had been a previous man whom she had dated very seriously, but she had never been convinced that a marriage with him would work out. When asked if she had ever changed her career plans because of such previous men, she explained:

No. And that was one of the bones of contention with this man that I say I dated seriously but was never convinced. I was determined that I would want to go on having my career. And what he wanted was what I used to call a nice Jewish housewife.

Rather than give up her career, she gave up the relationship.

One woman, although atypical, is of particular interest because she lived much of her adult life as a divorcee. The description of her life style when she was divorced — or, as she phrased it, when she was single — shows that such a life can have advantages for a professional woman. In discussing her eventual re-marriage, she said that just by a stroke of luck, she and her second husband were employed in the same area; had he been elsewhere, the situation would have been very difficult.

[Would you have moved if the man you wanted to marry did have to be in another city?] I liked being single. I abandoned it only after long thinking. I wasn't desirous of marrying again. . . . My career commitment was strong. I enjoyed it. I've worked all my life. This is how I chose to live my life. To abandon this for someone who has to be somewhere—well, if confronted with this, I just can't say.

Having spoken so positively of single life, she was asked to elaborate on what she saw as its advantages. Being single gave her more control over her own life. In her words, it was for "the most selfish of reasons — you do what you want when you want." Her one regret, in connection with single life, was not having had children. She said, "I regret it very much. But this is what happens, since my desire to have a child was not overwhelming enough to marry for that reason."

Her implication that she would have had a child only within marriage is of interest. Of course up to now, marriage has been required for parenthood to be socially acceptable. But now many people are experimenting with a variety of family structures and life styles. Variations are becoming more acceptable. It will be of interest to see whether single women will have and rear children if social definitions continue to change and they are "allowed" to do so. Several steps in the direction of single parenthood have already been taken. Adoption agencies in some places have changed their rules and now allow a single person of either sex to adopt. Also, more unwed mothers are keeping their babies rather than giving them up. These changing attitudes will undoubtedly increase the single woman's opportunities for fulfillment.

Though single life may be seen as desirable by the individual concerned, there is always the issue of how the status is viewed by others, or how one thinks it is viewed by others. One woman who had reservations about getting married, felt that students perceived her more favorably after her marriage.

The fact that I was single until my early thirties I think has affected my career in a positive way. . . . I think here at [the university] the fact that I am married—and I think [this is true] in general in dealing with young people, for a woman, anyhow—the fact that I am married, and have more or less of what is considered a normal life, evokes a favorable reaction from youngsters. I can talk about a lot of things, and they will believe me more than if I were not married. I was unmarried long enough to test that, you see. Maybe I wasn't an old old-maid, but you know (laughter), I was beginning to be considered one.

Whether the students' attitudes really changed or whether she just thought they did, this is still an example of the current stereotype that a woman is not seen as fulfilled without marriage and motherhood.

Was the Wife's Career Discussed Before Marriage?
One might expect a couple to discuss, prior to marriage, the issue of the wife's career. After all, having two careers in the family will pose many problems for them. Half the wives said they did discuss the issue. The position the wives took was that they wanted to continue their education and work. One of the more firm statements was:

I made the point—which he completely agreed with and obviously completely understood—that career was my way of life. And, that although I wanted a family also, I in no way considered this a matter of alternatives or substitutes, but a matter of both. And he completely agreed.

The other half of the wives reported that they did not discuss, prior to marriage, the issue of the wife's career. The reasons for lack of discussion of the issue varied. In a few early marriages, the women married first and became professionals later; that is, the wife did not have explicit career plans at the time she married. One said:

All of these sort of life decisions were not discussed, and, as I say, the whole thing of a career didn't present itself as a plan at that time.

In a few late marriages, the issue was not discussed because it was taken for granted that the wife would continue with her career. For example, one of these women said, "It was simply assumed. It was a simple matter of knowledge." They had known each other for a long time before marrying. And since he had a position similar to hers, she felt that she did not have to explain to him what having such a job meant. A few said they did not discuss their careers because it just was not their style to plan life so explicitly. One said that her husband planned his own life, but that she had never been capable of that. She said, "That's just not my style." Incidentally, this inattention to planning, on the part of some women, was not correlated with low involvement in career or lack of success. There were women who did not plan, but who were very committed to their work and very successful in it.

The men, although very much affected by being in a two-career family, had given little attention to the issue before meeting their wives. For example, the men were asked if, prior to meeting their wives, they had thought about whether they wanted to marry a woman primarily devoted to homemaking or a woman who had some career interests. Most men said that they had not thought about it, and only a few had explicitly considered the issue. Those who had thought about it said they preferred a woman with intellectual interests, with a professional orientation, or with a career of her own.

PARENTHOOD

The Desire for Children
In the view of most people in our society, marriage and children go together. Children have become obsolete as producers, and thus economic liabilities rather than assets. The reasons for wanting children may have changed, but people are still very much interested in having them. A survey done in the Detroit area shows the value placed on children. In the survey, almost all the couples wanted children. Marriages which were childless by choice were practically nonexistent. Further, wanting only one child was as rare as wanting none. The childless wives, except for recently married ones, expressed frustration over their fate. Thirty-six per cent of them could think of nothing good at all about the fact that they had not had children.[7]

Like most Americans, the professional couples placed a value on having children. Most of the wives said that having children was important to them and that they had expected to have them. This attitude was expressed not only by the mothers, but also by a couple of women who had remained childless. They said, "We wanted children, there was no doubt about it." "We definitely wanted a family." "We thought we should reproduce." Or, "I wanted a child intensely." For some, having children was unquestioned; it was just assumed. Only one woman, a mother, was completely negative about the idea of children; she saw no purpose in having them. Most of the men also said that they had wanted to have children. A few were rather neutral about the idea of fatherhood until the child actually was born, whereupon their enthusiasm grew. Only a few said that children were unimportant to them.

Although wanting to become mothers, a few of the women either had felt concern over how they would manage once the child was born or had felt hindered in their work during the pregnancy itself. One woman was finishing up some work in graduate school at the time, and said:

> *I got pregnant, and I was concerned for fear the schedule wouldn't work out. I mean I had these things to do and I didn't want this dratted baby to interfere with it.*

And another woman stressed the fatigue she experienced in the early months of pregnancy. She was so tired she could not get anything else done. She said, "I remember I was terribly discouraged at that time because it was cutting into everything — my whole way of life." For her, the fatigue passed after a couple of months and then she became quite happy about it. Because the above statements sound somewhat rejecting, perhaps it should be stressed once again that they were from women who in general had very positive attitudes toward motherhood and who were very devoted to their families.

Childbearing

Combining motherhood and career poses certain difficulties. It is not surprising that — despite their desire for children — these professional women differed both from the traditional wives and from the population as a whole in their actual childbearing patterns.

The life cycle of the family in the United States is more or less as follows. At first marriage, the husband is typically about twenty-two years old and his wife about twenty. The wife will bear her first child within about one and one half years after marriage. Young women now bear about 2.8 children in their lifetimes. They complete their childbearing, on the average, by age twenty-six or twenty-seven; this is about six years younger than their grandmothers were when they completed their families.[8]

In contrast, the childbearing of the professional women interviewed was atypical in three ways. First of all, they tended to have small families. Most (three quarters) of them had zero to two children. Secondly, there was likely to be a relatively long interval between marriage and birth of the first child. Not quite half of these wives had their first child within four years of marriage. Slightly over half waited five or more years before having their first child. Thirdly, most of the professional wives who were mothers had their first child at a relatively late age. Although most had their first child when they were in their twenties, usually it was in their late twenties. Furthermore, six wives were thirty-one years or older at the birth of their first child; indeed, one woman was thirty-six, and one was thirty-seven.[9]

Thus many of these professional women did not even *begin* their families until as late or later than the age at which women on the average *complete* their families. This suggests that it is age at birth of the first rather than the last child which is of greater relevance for women at the professional level. The question is, how established are the women in their careers prior to the time they also are responsible for the care of children. This focus is somewhat different from that usually found in the literature. Typically, attention has been given to the age of the mother at the birth of the last child, or when the last child enters school; and, the suggestion has often been made that since women are now completing their families earlier than in previous generations, they will therefore have additional years after the children are in school during which they can accept employment or engage in other activities outside the home. This line of thought does not seem to apply to the professional women interviewed; most worked even while raising a family. The difference between the two patterns of female employment — the nearly continuous and the severely interrupted — becomes important when one considers policy. Helping some women work when their children are young and helping other women return to the labor force after their children are in school would require two different types of institutional change.

The atypical childbearing patterns of professional women — found both in this and other studies — do not in themselves answer the question of whether "biology is destiny." A correlation, for example, between a small number of children and high involvement in career does not in itself tell you which of the following interpretations to choose. Is it that women who just happen to have few children are free to pursue careers? Or do women who want careers deliberately limit the size of their families? Nevertheless, a common approach by researchers has been to see how women's employment correlates with the composition of their families and then either to state or imply the "cause-effect" direction is that the composition of the woman's family determines whether or not she participates in the labor force. One example of this approach is provided by Eli Ginzberg, a professor of economics, in his study of educated women. He implies that the woman is passive in this process:

Children are the *primary* factor influencing a woman's work decisions. . . .

The data indicate that a woman's involvement in work will be determined first by her family situation and second by such factors as her educational achievement, her field of specialization, her location and her career plans.[10]

Ginzberg's approach has been attacked by Alice Rossi, a well known sociologist and advocate for women's rights. She criticizes Ginzberg for not raising the important possibility that things such as the kind of men these women married, where they lived, whether they had children or not and how many, are the *effects* of the values they held and the balance they wanted between work and family, rather than the *determinants* of their life styles.[11] The difference in interpretation is crucial. The issue at stake is whether women are passive in the process — at the mercy of their biology — or whether they actively influence their procreative function and adapt it to suit the kind of life style they want to lead.

With this issue in mind, the professional couples were asked about family planning. Their answers show the women were not necessarily at the mercy of their biology. Half the women with children reported that their career was one factor which influenced their childbearing. It influenced the size of their family or it influenced the timing and spacing of the children.

Some of these women were mostly concerned about how many children they had. For example, one woman explained the influence of her career on this as follows:

> *I've always thought that if I did not have a career, then I'd like a large family. . . . We jointly agreed two children at least. And we had a boy and a girl so now there's no need to have any more—especially because of our work load. We don't think we want one now because of work.*

Her husband stressed the time it took to bring up children. With both of them working, time was limited. He said that if they had more children, the proportion of time they could spend with each child would be less.

Other women were mostly concerned about when they had children. For example, in one couple the woman's career plans influenced the timing of her children in several ways. She said she had wanted a child intensely. She deferred having the first child with the notion that she would have it right after completing her professional education. Concerning the spacing of her children she stated:

> *We space them that way in terms of when I don't want to do anything else. I make calculated guesses of when I can get time off. I calculate on*

time off before *I get pregnant — I mention that in ten months or so there may be a child coming and see what can be arranged.*

Her husband commented more about postponing the first child. "It was eight or nine years before the first child and we were well established. . . . When we were established, then we decided we'd try one."

The women's logic of what would be most beneficial for their careers was not always the same. For example, one woman spaced her children with several years in between, fitting pregnancies into her work schedule. But another woman had all her children close together because she felt she would be freer if the children had each other for companionship.

For some women, the importance they attached to controlling pregnancy varied over time and depended on what was happening in their professional life. The following quote is interesting in this connection. This woman described how at one point in her career she was established and holding a secure job so it was not necessary to plan her family in terms of her career. But later, in a less secure job, she became concerned about controlling the timing of her pregnancy.

We had decided with the first child that we very much wanted to have a child and that I would simply take a chance, whenever the pregnancy would occur. I suppose I would have to say that I was on tenure in my post at the time, and I was very well known and established there and I realized that if anything did go wrong—say I had to miss school for a month—why this would be called standard sick leave. I had no concern about problems. When we planned our second child, however, which was just after we came here, such was not the case; and I timed the pregnancy so that it could occur only with a summer birth. I didn't want to take that sort of gamble. And fortunately everything went well.

The fact that careers were, for some women, one factor in planning their families indicates that women do not necessarily lead life styles that are merely the result of how many children they have. The experiences of these twenty professional women suggest that the correlations researchers find between family composition and labor force participation of women may be due to two opposite processes. On the one hand, there were a few women who had fewer children than desired because of physical problems and who expressed very ambivalent attitudes about working mothers. They suffered miscarriages, were unable to conceive at all or for as many times as desired, or suffered prolonged illness during and because of the first pregnancy. It would appear that for these few women it is their inadventently limited families which have allowed them to work as much as they have. On the other hand, there were eight women in which the "cause-effect" went in the opposite direction. These eight planned their childbearing partially in terms of their careers.[12]

The Childless Wives

There were only four childless wives among the twenty professional women. All four expressed some regrets about this fact. It was a sacrifice; they would have enjoyed children. The two who were childless because of biological reasons had both considered adoption. But each gave several reasons for not having followed through with an adoption; for example, ambivalence about rearing a child, not being considered appropriate prospective parents by adoption agencies' criteria, involvement in career. One explained her situation as follows:

> *We talked of adopting, but it would have been such a chore because my husband isn't [the same religion] and because of our age. We would have had two major strikes against us, so that would mean scrounging around and not being able to adopt through a regular agency. Plus the fact that we were already beginning to be somewhat ambivalent. So it just meant taking enormous initiative and I think that's what one has to do if you're going to adopt. . . . We didn't really explore it the way younger couples often do.*

This quote shows how adoption agencies, by accepting ideas prevalent in the society about who makes good parents, make it harder for couples like these to adopt. Or, at the very least, such rules play into people's psychological problems if they are ambivalent about having children.

The regrets of the four childless women, however, seem to have been tempered by other satisfactions and interests in life. The most ambivalent of the four explained her situation as follows. One of the reasons she married was because she thought she wanted kids. But then she just did not get pregnant.

> *But, you know, I was 39 when I got married so I was already very ambivalent. . . . I began to wonder more and more, whether I would really be able to be tolerant and be able to handle all the responsibilities of a small child. . . . I don't think it's been as major a disappointment as I might one day in the past have thought it would be. . . . If there's one thing I've missed, by marrying late, it's that. My major regret I guess would be that I haven't had kids. But I don't feel very sad about it.*

In general, the comments of these childless wives were in keeping with the findings reported in a recent study of women who had never married. Luther Baker, a professor of family life, administered personality tests to women who had never married and to women who were married and had children. The tests showed that these two groups were very similar to each other in their personal and social adjustment. His conclusion was that personal fulfillment does not depend on marriage and parenthood. The unmarried women, for example, did not express feelings of "not being a whole person" because they were single. "Their sense of personal worth comes not from their biological function as a female but from their social function as a human being, from what they perceive as a creative contribution to their significant society."[13] The women in both groups were selected from Business and Professional Women's Clubs. In searching for an explanation of the similarity of their adjustment, Baker notes that women in both groups listed work at the top of their sources of personal accomplishment and satisfaction. He cautions against generalizing to women without such creative jobs. His caution is probably justified. Childless wives in a survey of families in the Detroit area stressed the negative aspects of their situation. Above all, they missed the companionship children would have provided. They emphasized the loneliness of being a childless wife.[14]

THE TRADITIONAL COUPLES

The traditional couples — especially the women — saw the woman's role as oriented more exclusively toward marriage and children. This can be seen both in their actual childbearing patterns and in the attitudes they expressed.

Even these traditional wives began their families relatively late. They all had their first child when they were in their late twenties. But whereas six professional wives were over thirty at the birth of their first child, none of the traditional wives waited this long. Professional wives were more likely to wait a longer number of years than traditional wives between marriage and birth of their first child. Not quite half the professional wives had their first child within four years of marriage. Almost all the traditional wives had their first child within this amount of time; the sole exception was one case where the woman's first child died at birth and thus her first surviving child was not born within four years of marriage. Most of the professional wives had zero to two children. In contrast, all the traditional wives had two or more children.

In general, the traditional women seemed more exclusively oriented to the family and less concerned about what effect a family would have on their career. Prior to marriage, these couples tended not to discuss the issue of the wife's career. All the traditional women married while in their twenties, and if they got divorced, they remarried while still in their twenties. Late marriage where the wife was thirty or over did not occur. One woman said, "Marriage for me had priority. The best thing was to get married and then think about professional life later." All traditional women reported that they simply assumed that they would have children or that having children was important to them in their present marriage. Most of their husbands also took this view. Only one woman expressed any career-related regrets over being pregnant. Hardly any of these women reported that their career was a factor influencing how many children they had or when they had them. There was one woman who had hoped to finish her graduate education before having children, but did not do so; she said if she thought about it at all, it was in terms of, "I must get this damn Ph.D. finished so that I can have my kids." And there was one other woman who began to think in these terms — but only after having children and returning to school.

The comments of a few traditional wives are interesting in that they imply that involvement in a large family and involvement in a career may serve as alternatives to each other. One said:

> *I suppose if I had embarked on a serious career of my own at an earlier age, I wouldn't have wanted, wouldn't have needed, to have a spread-out family or so much of a family.*

This woman solved the problem of what to do with her life by having more children. Another solved it the opposite way. After three children, she and her husband felt that was all they could manage. It was depressing to her to think that her family was finished. To overcome the depression, she began to do other things. And this was one of the factors that got her back to work. To the extent that women see work and continued childbearing as alternate sources of satisfaction, the implications for people worried about the world's population explosion should be obvious.

A few traditional women expressed considerable pleasure in feeling needed by the family and having others dependent upon them. Like the others who had been away from their careers, these two were asked if they felt any lack of confidence because of rusty skills. They did worry over the adequacy of their professional knowledge and abilities, but they also said that they felt more confident in another way after having a family. As one said:

> *I wished to get married and I found in marriage certain things that I was looking for. . . . Before I was married, I felt a different kind of lack of confidence in myself which I don't have any more now that I am married and have the children and so on and have so many (laughter) people depending on me in some way.*

She implied that she now had a greater feeling of security as a woman. And, as so many traditional women, she gave greater priority — both in word and in deed — to the domestic role than to the career.

NOTES

1. The pervasiveness of these stereotypes is reported by Baker. He also questions them. Luther G. Baker, Jr., "The Personal and Social Adjustment of the Never-Married Woman," *Journal of Marriage and the Family*, 30 (August, 1968), pp. 473-79.

2. Theodore Caplow, *The Sociology of Work*, "Occupations of Women" (New York: McGraw-Hill, 1964), p. 244. (First published in 1954: University of Minnesota.)

3. *Ibid.*

4. Margaret Hennig, "Career Development for Women Executives" (unpublished Doctor of Business Administration dissertation, Harvard University, 1970), p. VII-10 and p. VI-15.

5. Helen S. Astin, *The Woman Doctorate in America: Origins, Career, and Family* (New York: Russell Sage Foundation, 1969), p. 26. Another survey, done of people who received doctorates between 1958 and 1963 reports that 50% of the women married, in contrast to over 95% of the men. Rita James Simon, Shirley Merritt Clark, and Kathleen Galway, "The Woman Ph.D.: A Recent Profile," *Social Problems*, 15 (Fall, 1967), p. 222.

6. The occasions of laughter are reported because they occurred in patterned ways throughout the interviews. They were most often associated with problems or hard times, a point of tension, an earlier naive view, or an opinion at variance with others.

7. Robert O. Blood, Jr. and Donald M. Wolfe, *Husbands and Wives: The Dynamics of Married Living* (New York: Free Press, 1960), p. 137.

8. It is difficult to make exact comparisons with the general population at any given point in time because when interviewed in 1968, the women in the present study ranged in age from 35 to 55. Nevertheless, comparison with the figures presented here gives some indication of how they differ from the

general population. The figures are taken from Goode and he relies heavily on Glick's analysis of 1950 census data. William J. Goode, *The Family* (Englewood Cliffs, New Jersey: Prentice-Hall, 1964), p. 68. For more precise and detailed information see Paul C. Glick, *American Families*, "The Life Cycle of the Family" (New York: Wiley, 1957), pp. 53-70.

9. Other studies have reported similar deviations between the childbearing of professional women and those of the general female population. For example, Astin found that the married woman doctorate was more apt to be childless than her counterpart in the general population, her family was smaller (she had an average of two children), and her childbearing started and terminated much later. Astin, *op. cit.*, pp. 29-31.

10. Eli Ginzberg with Associates, *Life Styles of Educated Women* (New York: Columbia University Press, 1966), pp. 82-84. As another example see Astin who states that "the number and ages of her children and her husband's income are important determinants of the woman doctorate's decisions regarding employment." Astin, *op. cit.*, p. 67.

11. Alice S. Rossi, "Review of Ginzberg: Life Styles of Educated Women," *American Sociological Review*, 31 (December, 1966), pp. 874-75.

12. Among the twenty there were also some women who saw the issue as completely irrelevant.

13. Baker, *op. cit.*, p. 478.

14. Blood and Wolfe, *op. cit.*, pp. 137-38.

4

The Inflexibility of Occupations

*We just accept [traveling]. We
don't ever have to be away very
long. . . . If I go, it's perhaps a week
or ten days.*

Professional wife

*I suggested that I was going to go
to . . . these meetings. . . . And
he was astounded! He said, "You
know, you're not going to go and
leave me, are you?"*

Traditional wife

The trouble with having a profession today is that if you have one, you
are expected to pursue it in a certain way — and it is a very rigid way.
You are supposed to move when the call of the profession tells you to
move, even if it is clear across the country. And you are supposed to
stay put when it calls upon you to stay put. Many employers will not
hire your spouse if they employ you, and will not hire you if they employ your spouse. You must have a professional address — a formally
acceptable place of employment — in order to be considered a practicing member by the world at large. And you are expected to show
single-minded devotion to career, placing it above all other interests in
life.

Every single one of these current expectations has behind it the
assumption that there will be only one career in the family and that
interests of other family members will be subordinated to it. If both
husband and wife have professions, it is nearly impossible for them to
meet the expectations exactly as they are outlined above. Instead they
must compromise and innovate. And that is what this chapter is about.

A NATION OF ITINERANTS

The occupational pressures for mobility and immobility often constitute a major barrier for the two-career family. It is advantageous for career advancement if a person can decide where to live without taking into account the interests of other members of the family. Most often, it is a question of being mobile. It is an advantage to be able to move about, for there are more job opportunities if a person is not restricted to one locale. There are more employment and advancement opportunities if one becomes an itinerant and goes from employer to employer.[1] Furthermore, for some jobs, an individual is expected to move even to retain the same job or stay with the same employer.

The opposite of mobility is also important. At times a person needs to be able to remain in one place long enough to finish school, to fulfill a job commitment that he has made, or to pursue professional advancement at a given place. He or she cannot afford to be taken away to some other place just because some other family member has to move.

The rules now are made for the person who can decide where to live independently of family ties. This relationship between geographic mobility and the family has been analyzed by the well-known social theorist Talcott Parsons. He states that since occupations so often require an individual to shift his place of residence, it is essential to have the type of family that is able to move too. This, Parsons believes, requires having a small isolated family which is not bound to a particular residential locale by interests, such as career, property, or status concerns, or other members of the family.[2]

This means that the rules are now made for men. The so-called "solution" to the problem of geographic mobility has been to make men mobile and to discourage women from the pursuit of a serious career at all. This statement applies especially to married women. However, since most women expect to marry, the practical effect of discouraging married women is to discourage almost all of them. By not permitting the wife to have competing career interests, existing social patterns free her to follow her husband on his itinerant circuit of jobs.

In the two-career family the situation is more complex. It would be to each spouse's advantage to decide where to live without taking into account the other's interests; career opportunities may beckon them in opposite directions. Yet presumably the husband and wife wish to remain together as a family. The difficulty of both partners finding suitable employment in the same area has been analyzed by sociologist Philip Slater. He sees that there are great advantages to wives having careers of their own. However, he also sees that there would be strains, especially if geographic mobility increases in the future. "At any moment competing job requirements or opportunities might threaten to separate the couple geographically. This is an increasing problem in the academic world, where more and more professional couples are appearing. Unless the wife is willing to assume ancillary status it is often difficult for the couple both to find desirable positions in the same community."[3] Thus it is clear that the one-career family fits into the present occupational system more easily than the two-career family does.

Although mobility is discussed here mainly from the point of view of occupational pressures to move, it should be noted that there is a paradox involved for the family. Mobility threatens to separate the couple with two careers; the partners may feel drawn in different directions. But studies of the family show that it is conditions of mobility which heighten the importance of the marital relationship in the first place. When a couple moves about, the marriage partners leave other relationships behind and thus increase the emotional demands they place on each other.[4] Thus the same process — mobility — both heightens the importance of the marital relationship and threatens to disrupt this relationship.

All the couples interviewed were asked how they dealt with the career pressures to move. The professional couples are first discussed below. Their way of handling the issue was very different from that of the traditional couples who are discussed later.

Where to Live

Most of the professional couples reported that the issue of moving had arisen since their marriage. Specifically, fifteen of the twenty said this had occurred, and the discussion here is based on their comments.

In every single one of these cases at least once the wife's decision about where to live was significantly influenced by the career needs of her husband. In most of these cases, the decision was to move. And then the couple either negotiated simultaneously for a set of positions, moved taking account of the occupational needs of both people, or the wife followed the husband. In a few of these cases the wife was unable — or unwilling — to move. She was restricted to one place, tied to a husband who could not — would not — ever move. But these couples still had to deal with the mobility issue because career possibilities existed elsewhere for the wife. This influence of the husband's career on the wife is not surprising. It is very much in keeping with the present expectation that a wife should follow her husband and that his work should be the determinant of where they choose to live.

Turning the question around, however, there is a much more interesting finding. In most of these same couples at least once the husband's decision about where to live was significantly influenced by his wife's career. This happened specifically in twelve of the fifteen cases. In most of these twelve cases, a move occurred. The couple negotiated simultaneously for a set of positions, they moved taking account of the occupational needs of both people, or the husband actually followed the wife. In a few of the twelve cases, the decision was not to move or to postpone a move; the husband remained somewhere an additional length of time while the wife finished up something, such as course work or a research project, that she was doing. This influence of the wife's career on the husband is of greater interest. It is quite a departure from middle-class norms, and it is something that previous studies have not paid much attention to. They usually have emphasized only the opposite finding.

A Set of Two Positions

There were four couples in which the husband and wife successfully negotiated for a set of two positions from one employer. In three of these cases, negotiations either involved the husband first or both people right from the beginning. In one case, the original offer clearly was made to the wife. She and her husband were in very different fields; they had never worked together professionally and had not been viewed as a team. She said she could not accept unless a position could be found for her husband too.

> I said yes I would be very interested. It sounded like just the thing that anybody working in [my field] would enjoy. But I felt that it was out of the question since they would have to find a job for my husband. . . . And I forgot about it, and thought well it was a nice thing, but it's one of those things, if you're going to combine marriage and career you can't always have things your own way. Well, the man . . . was interested enough to pursue the matter, said there has to be something, it's a big university. . . . By a series of circumstances it turned out that [another position became vacant]. . . . I don't think these things happen too often. This was just a series of circumstances; the pieces just seemed to fall together.

This case illustrates several other general points. Hiring a couple as a package deal may create problems for the employer. First of all, there is the question of whether he needs or can use two such people. In other words, what is the probability that one employer needs two people with the precise combination of skills offered by a husband and wife? This dilemma has nothing to do with discrimination; it is more a question of the statistical probability of manpower requirements. The woman, in the case quoted above, implied that it was fortunate that the institution in question was a large one which employed many people in diverse fields. Secondly, hiring a "person plus a spouse" may create extra work for the employer. He must go out of his way to find positions for both people. He must be interested enough in the potential employee to do this. An applicant who must also obtain a job for his or her spouse is usually competing against other applicants who do not pose this additional problem for the employer.

There is some indication that it is easier for couples to demand a set of positions as they get better known and as their professional reputations go up. For example, these four couples were not necessarily successful in getting a set of positions the first time they moved. In fact, some comments made in the interviews indicated their belief that it had become easier with time. One husband described as follows how he and his wife have come to make it known that they move only on the condition that they both get appointments:

> *I resist very strongly this view which is very prevalent in this country that if you're dealing with husband and wife it's always natural to offer the husband something. And so it became well known in this country long ago that [the Smiths] were not prepared to do things except on this condition [that we both get appointments]. And as we became, you know, as we got better known, these things of course became easier to arrange. . . . Now we're both in the same department and we both have full-time professorships.*

If the husband and wife are in the same or related fields, and if they work together at least part of the time, they may establish a reputation as a team. This occurred in the above case. And the wife in another couple also explained her situation this way:

> *I don't solicit these [offers] because with a husband-wife team, it's been accepted that if the husband moves, the wife goes along too. . . . It's understood. We both agreed we wouldn't accept an offer where there would be a job for only one person. We both had been invited to ——— university and also to ———. We were both invited simultaneously. . . . Whenever we make a change, we have always requested two positions. ·*

In viewing the fact that four couples did negotiate successfully for sets of positions, it should be emphasized that in the occupational world as a whole, this type of employment pattern is very rare.

Relative Weight Given to Each Spouse's Career
For many couples, the issue of moving arose not just once, but again and again. Thus to understand the relative weight a couple gave to each

partner's career, one has to look at how they resolved not just one decision but a whole series of decisions about where to live. In about half the cases, the relative weight given to the husband's vs. the wife's career changed as they made a series of decisions about where to live; at some point there was something particularly compelling about one spouse's career needs, and later the situation was reversed. In a few couples the husband's career needs clearly dominated their decisions about where to live, although some consideration was also given to the wife. In a few cases, the husband's career not only dominated where they lived but made the couple immobile; the man's work was firmly rooted in one area and he was unwilling to move, even though opportunities existed elsewhere for the wife. The details of these three types of couples are given blow.

In half the cases, as mentioned above, a given couple did not resolve each decision about where to live in the same way. The relative weight they gave to each spouse's career changed as they made a series of decisions about geographic residence. The "Wilsons" are an example of this type of couple. The Wilsons are in different fields; he is a physical scientist and she a social scientist. When interviewed, they were employed by different universities. They originally met each other toward the end of their graduate schooling. After marrying, they moved four times. The first time, Mrs. Wilson was going abroad to do research, and for Mr. Wilson, who also had to go abroad at some time, his choice of when to go was very much influenced by when his wife was going. The second time they moved, Mr. Wilson was supposed to go one place to begin post-graduate work, and Mrs. Wilson was supposed to go elsewhere to finish up graduate school. He got his appointment postponed, and they moved to the city where she was in school. In the third change, they moved for his appointment. She started looking for a job only after they arrived in this next city. At the time of the fourth move, the Wilsons were both looking for more permanent employment. Mr. Wilson's decision was influenced by his wife's career: he turned down a job offer in an isolated town where there was only one university and no opportunities for her, he turned down another offer where she would have had a very long commute to work. Finally, he accepted a job in a metropolitan area where there appeared to be more opportunities for her. Mrs. Wilson began job hunting before the actual move. She did not actually secure a position herself before they definitely decided to move. She subsequently found a job at an institution which had been on her list of ten preferred places in the area. However, she said that if there had been no opening at any of these ten, she would have tried the next ten places on her list.

This case history of the Wilsons provides an example of how the relative weight given to each spouse's career may change from move to move. We consider the case in some detail because, in addition, it happens to illustrate several other general patterns which occurred frequently among the professional couples. First of all, there can be moves in which one finds simultaneously that the husband takes account of where the wife can work, but the wife still follows the husband. On the Wilsons' last move, Mr. Wilson moved to a metropolis where his wife could work, but he secured a position first. Secondly, if one spouse takes a risk, it is usually the wife who does so. This point will be elaborated on later. In this particular case, Mrs. Wilson took a risk by moving before she had definitely secured a position. Thirdly, the husband's career decisions may be influenced by the wife's career more than has been recognized in most career studies. Fourth, despite the best intentions on the part of both husband and wife, at least one partner, usually the wife, may still make career sacrifices when choosing where to live. In this particular case, Mrs. Wilson went down a list she had made of potential employers until she found a job. She accepted employment at a school which did not have graduate students even though she would have enjoyed teaching graduates.

In a few couples the husband's career clearly dominated their decisions about where to live, although consideration was also given to the wife's career. These decisions tended to be reported differently by the husband and the wife. Their accounts did not contradict one another. But they did show a difference in emphasis. The husband stressed that they took into account the wife's situation when deciding when or where to move. The wife stressed that she followed her husband. The following quotes, both from one couple, illustrate this subtle difference in perception.

> *We had talked about the way of finding a new opportunity and all of our conversation involved the question of where could we find opportunity for both of us, professional opportunity. So that our concern was always with the kind of locale, the kind of venue, where there would be more schools than one, where she could herself find her opportunity without being involved in the same school. . . . I must say that her attitude was that if the job interests me, if it seems good, that would be enough for the present, that sooner or later, we would find our way as far as she's concerned.*
> *(husband's interview)*

> *Well in the first place our first consideration was to choose an area with more than one college available. . . . We decided also that since my husband was a full professor and at the peak of his career, and I was on a different level in a sense, that we would let him get the job knowing that*

it was an area where eventually I could get a job too. . . . We agreed that he would get the job and that I would follow, and this was because of his advanced rank.

(wife's interview)

The husband is saying that, unlike many men, he has gone out of his way to help his wife. The wife is saying that even with a considerate husband, a woman often has to take second place.

In a few cases, the wives were unable or unwilling to move although opportunities for them did exist elsewhere. These were three women who married men with careers firmly rooted in one locale. These women knew, even at the time of marriage, that their husbands' work would not enable the husbands to leave. The women recognized that this would be a limitation professionally. One woman described this limitation and her feelings about it as follows:

> *I have had the feeling over and over again, practically every year, around contract time, that perhaps I wouldn't have stayed here. Not now anymore, I mean, now I'm a full professor and I'm pretty settled and old enough to be willing to help fight out the problems that there are here because they exist everywhere. And I'm willing to devote myself to [this university]. But for a number of years I felt a little tied down. . . . There is really very little in the area. . . . I know I could move out a little bit if I were willing to be away two or three days a week and come back. I'm very much devoted to my home and to my husband, and we got married late, and I just feel that I don't want to spend two or three days away.*

Another woman described how she reconciled this dilemma in her mind even prior to marrying a man who she knew would not be able to move.

> *[How do you feel about the fact your husband can't move?] Well, this is what I figured all out before we got married. If I had not been willing to stay put [here] for the rest of my life, I wouldn't have married him. So that was all settled a long time ago.*

The three men whose occupations held them to one area described the chronology of their careers without much reference to their wife's career. In contrast, men who had made moves in which the wife's career was a factor included this information when giving an account of their own careers.

Where Can the Occupation Be Practiced
The extent to which an occupation can be practiced anywhere is an important factor. There are occupations, such as free-lance writing,

which can be done almost any place. At the other extreme, there are occupations which can be practiced in only one or a few locales. High fashion models, national politicians, and Sanskrit specialists have a very limited number of places where they can follow their trade.

Most men and women in the professional couples interviewed have had considerable leeway and were able to practice their occupation in a variety of places. There were, however, a few people who were either restricted to one place or had only a very limited number of places where they could work because of the special features of their profession. They needed access to specialized libraries or equipment, owned a local business, or had an established local clientele. There were the three husbands, mentioned previously, who could not move. There was also one couple where both the husband and wife were limited because they both needed access to special archives. As the husband explained:

> *The serious job considerations have really always been in the area. If we would move to any place else, it's a very difficult thing to decide because it means, you know, giving up my library, also it means giving up her library.*

And another couple's moves had been influenced by the wife's need to use highly specialized and expensive equipment. In her field, a person with access to certain big instruments could work on many scientific problems that others could not tackle. This equipment constituted a scarce resource in the profession; indeed, the shortage of this type of equipment caused a bottleneck in the profession and limited the number of people who could do this type of work.

The Wife Takes the Risk

If someone takes a risk when deciding where to live, it is almost always the wife who does so. The most common form of risk taking occurs when a couple moves before the wife has job-hunted or before she has definitely secured a position. Occasionally some other type of employment risk is incurred. For example, in one couple interviewed the wife took a chance by agreeing to marry a man who could not move elsewhere; she knew that she was making herself geographically immobile, she did not have a permanent position at the time and was not even sure that she could attain such a position without moving. In another couple, the husband and wife simultaneously moved to a university that had higher academic standards than the place where they were previously employed. The husband was hired with tenure. The wife, however, took a risk in moving because of the stricter academic regulations; she not only had to take a step down in position until the completion of her degree; but, there was also uncertainty as to whether she would be able to attain tenure at the second university. Fortunately, she later did.

The Wife Sacrifices More
One can ask where a man or woman would have gone if he or she did not have to take account of the other person's career? Is there a lowering of ambitions? Has the person lowered his or her professional choices in order to accommodate to the other partner's career? Looking at the couples from this point of view, it is obvious that many husbands were restricted in the sense that they went out of their way to live in places where their wives could also obtain employment. Yet it was still the wives who typically made the greater career sacrifices when deciding where to live. Among the couples interviewed it was the women who accommodated to their husband's careers more than vice versa. It was wives, not husbands, who gave up a permanent position with no new position yet in sight, stepped back when anti-nepotism rules were imposed, interrupted their graduate education in order to move for the other person's job, or restricted themselves to this country despite a desire to work abroad. As we shall see, this same pattern of accommodation occurred on other issues too.

The Desirability of the Offer
The attractiveness of a move or offer for career advancement is an important factor. The extremes are the most interesting: moves in which there is a great deal to be gained or a great deal lost. On the one hand, the people interviewed occasionally mentioned, hypothetically, the possibility of getting an outstanding offer — something so tempting and unusual that one would be unlikely to turn it down. On the other hand, there was often a lower limit beyond which the wife would not agree to move. This was most often expressed as an unwillingness to move to a place where there were no opportunities for her — for example, to an isolated place or a place with only one employer. Occasionally this lower limit was stated more specifically; for instance, one wife refused to move to the west coast because it would be too far away from the source of data for her research.

Discrimination Against Women Also Affects Men
This discussion on geographic residence has been presented primarily in terms of the structural difficulty of finding two jobs in one area. But the attitudinal factor of discrimination against women is also important. Discrimination — or indeed any factor which makes it harder

for the wife to find employment — also makes it harder for a couple to find employment together. Occasionally the persons interviewed reported experiencing blatant discrimination or openly hostile attitudes toward women. For example, one wife described the possibility of a move back to a place where she and her husband had been before, and where she had been discriminated against. In describing the factors which made the couple decide against the return, the wife included as one reason "the problem of women not being welcome there." Another wife described her experience of applying to graduate school; discrimination against women was one factor which influenced where she and her first husband chose to attend school.

We got a letter back saying that I would have to register and be part of a women's college; the university did not grant Ph.D.'s to women. This put my back up, so we went to [the other university].

Thus discrimination against women influenced both of their careers.

The Employer's View
The employer's perception of the two-career family is another important factor. Is the employer even aware of the fact that the person's career plans may be influenced by the career interests of the other marriage partner? And if he is aware of the situation, then what is his attitude toward it?[5]

Chance comments by people interviewed suggest that in the future it might be profitable to investigate employers' attitudes on a whole range of issues relevant to the two-career family. Obviously, employers must take the marriage into account in cases where anti-nepotism rules are involved or when a couple requests a set of two positions. But there were people interviewed who also felt that the employer took cognizance of the marriage when the husband and wife were to be employed in different institutions. For example, a few women said they felt that they had been taken advantage of because the employer knew they were geographically immobile. One was a woman whose husband worked nearby and it was known that he had no intention of leaving. When asked if her employer had taken account of her family obligations — in context, the question implied receiving a favor — she began her answer with an account of the opposite.

Well, first let me put it the other way around because that was the sore point. I would say this for everybody — everybody was very frank and honest and openly admitted that they were taking advantage of me because they knew I was stuck in the area. . . . So in that sense I feel that

I have sometimes been taken advantage of. [In terms of time or salary or what?] Salary mainly. Also in terms of coming up for tenure. I was due up for tenure and there were two men who had come after I had, but the department was very eager to keep them and, you know, I was asked if I would wait a year. And I waited a year and let the two men get tenure before I did. One has since left.

In another case, a husband had recently been in the position of hiring a man whose career decisions were influenced by the profession of his wife. The issue of a husband and wife getting jobs was discussed with this man not only from the point of view of his own private life as a job applicant, but also from his vantage point as an employer of other such couples. He reported that in his role as employer he suddenly had a new perspective when he himself needed to hire a man who would stay a while. The fact that the career interests of the applicant's wife might influence the applicant, made it seem a bit risky to hire him. In the employer's view, the career interests of the wife posed an unknown factor; he worried about what would happen if the wife, after a year, did not like the area professionally and wanted to move elsewhere. This case suggests that in a future study of the two-career family, one might ask more explicitly what — if anything — people told potential employers about the spouse's profession.

The Pattern in the Professional Couples

We have seen how finding two jobs near each other can constitute a major problem for the two-career family. No matter how favorable attitudes are on the part of the husband, wife, and employers, in practical terms it may still be difficult for the couple to secure desirable employment for both. The interviews show that both marriage partners may be affected by this dilemma. The wives accommodated to their husbands' careers, more than vice versa, when deciding where to live. But the more surprising finding is how much the husbands' decisions were affected by the career interests of their wives. In quite a departure from middle-class norms, many husbands went out of their way to live in places where their wives could also obtain desirable employment.

The Traditional Couples

Unlike the pattern in the professional couples, the husband's career clearly dominated the traditional couples' decisions of where to live. For all the traditional couples, his career was of paramount importance in their choice of residence, and in only two of the seven couples interviewed was the wife's career even a factor at all.

The traditional couples all had faced the issue of whether to move since the time of their marriage, and almost all had actually moved at least once. The wife followed her husband on his itinerant circuit of jobs. Her career either was not a factor or was a very minor factor. Some moves occurred at a point in the family life cycle when the husband and wife believed that she had no career interests. This relates to the fact that most traditional wives withdrew from their careers much longer for child rearing than the professional wives did. For example, one traditional couple had made several previous moves in which no thought was given to her professional life. She described their most recent move in terms of the husband's career; then when asked how she felt about the move, she stated:

> Oh I was delighted . . . from every point of view. From the point of view for his own work, this was much more interesting. For the education of our children this was much more interesting. . . . Also I knew that Boston was a major center of intellectual life of all kinds. . . . I really didn't think about my professional life at that point. I just thought well it will be a much more lively intellectual atmosphere and there'll be much more things worthwhile and later on, should we stay there for some length of time, I'll be able to find something worth doing too.

The husband, citing factors involved in this decision, mentioned his work, the education of the children, and the desire for an interesting place to live. Only after lengthy discussion of these three factors did he mention that in the future they envisioned her returning to some kind of job; but he did not see this specifically as one of the reasons for the move.

This case also shows that a husband and wife may make a decision jointly and still not consider the wife's career interests to be relevant to the decision. In this particular couple, her career was not a factor, but both told how they discussed the move with each other. The husband said, "It was a joint decision all along." The wife's situation was so merged with that of her husband that she spoke of whether "we" got an offer, though technically, of course, only "he" got an offer. Thus the issue of living where both marital partners could obtain suitable jobs — an issue very much on the minds of many professional couples — was hardly mentioned at all by most traditional couples. If it was mentioned, it was sort of as an afterthought.

In a few traditional couples, the fact that a wife's career might be relevant was seen very negatively by the husband. One husband said that if it ever seemed a good idea to move for *his* career, then there was no question that they would move. He felt that "what was best for the family was what was best for the major breadwinner's career." He said he would be *very* unhappy if his wife had a career that might influence where she would be willing to live. Another man deliberately did not marry a career wife. He spoke negatively of a friend whose situation he perceived as follows:

> *I know of a third case, another good friend of ours. I think actually his career decisions have been made essentially because of his wife's career decisions, not his own. . . . I think he made a dreadful mistake in not taking offers to go elsewhere; here's another example of this kind of conflict. . . . That's why I've never allowed [my wife's work] to reach that point (laughter) and my wife has never wanted it to reach that point.*

In only two traditional couples, were the career interests of the wife ever taken into account when moving. Even so, one such wife sacrificed a great deal. The negative aspects of the move were paramount in her mind:

> *During this time my husband decided to move us. . . . I think it may mean I won't get my degree. It's not that it's impossible, but there is a kind of cumulative fatigue that sets in when you struggle with a problem year after year. . . . Since we've been here I've had serious doubts about the whole question of women having careers. It seems like an extremely fragile arrangement which the slightest thing can knock over. . . . I am in a state of acute conflict over having a career. . . . I don't know if I can, if I ought, if I want to finish. These issues are all open again because of the move.*

Only after considerable discussion along this line, did the woman even acknowledge that her husband first had looked for jobs that would not have involved a move. Judging from both their accounts, the problem was compounded by a very superficial understanding on his part. Throughout his interview he showed very little awareness of, or sympathy for, the problems his wife experienced. For example, he talked only briefly — and flippantly — about their recent move. All he would say was, "She regrets in some respects moving. She lost some professional relationships." The case suggests that it is not only the factors of making a move or making a sacrifice that are important. In addition, the manner in which the move comes about may reveal how much or how little the husband really cares about his wife's career interests. A cavalier attitude merely adds insult to injury.

GLOBE-TROTTING: TRAVEL AND SEPARATIONS

In addition to the numerous changes of residence discussed previously, professional jobs frequently require a great deal of short-term mobility and travel. Meetings, conferences, lectures, traveling to get information, and consulting are all part of professional life today.

These patterns, too, are easier for the person who can get about without having to worry over the family. It is assumed that the man can leave the family behind — the wife will be there to tend the home fires. And it is assumed that the man can ask his wife to accompany him if he chooses — she will not have interests of her own which prevent this. Obviously, these current expectations pose a barrier for the two-career family.

Travel

It is clear that as least occasionally a person with a profession will be required to travel alone. The professional couples were asked about these types of trips, and especially about the wife's travel, since one would expect that to be the most problematical. Historically women have been tied to hearth and home, excluded from mobile pursuits, such as hunting, by the encumbrances of pregnancy, childbirth, and child rearing.[6] Their general immobility has been shown in cross-cultural research on the division of labor by sex. Mobility is a major principle which universally distinguishes men's from women's tasks. Though this generalization is breaking down in modern society, the stereotype still persists.

When seen against this background, the amount of travel done by the professional wives is remarkable. Most of the wives did travel on brief business trips without their husbands. These journeys alone lasted from two to ten days. In addition, two wives also made regular airplane commutes once a month. One went on a regular schedule to gather data for her research; the other one flew to a nearby city to attend a monthly seminar. Both were mothers and each still had a school-age child at home. Even more remarkable, six of the twenty wives went alone to Europe, Africa, or Asia on extended trips. They were gone anywhere from three weeks to almost a year. In the longest of these separations, the family was periodically reunited. Five of these six women had children, pre-schoolers or school-age youngsters, at the time of their extended journeys, and the children remained with the husband while the wife was away. In a few couples, both the husband and wife went abroad, and then separated and went to different countries; again, as they went their separate ways, the children stayed with the husband.

Almost all the men traveled alone on business, as might be expected. The general trend was that the husband traveled more than the wife; however, there were a few couples in which this pattern was reversed. No woman traveled alone the "excessive amount" that a few men did

— away on the average of two months each year or covering 60,000 miles per year. No woman traveled at the beck and call of the employer, with only minimal control over when and where she went, but a few men did travel under such conditions. One woman, however, did travel alone to territory regarded as potentially dangerous. She reported that she limited her travel somewhat because of the danger. She said if she did not have the children she would go more often and she would take more risks going.

The Long-Distance Commute

When career opportunities beckon in opposite directions, one possible solution is a long-distance commute. You can divide the family during the week and get it back together on the weekends. This may be the answer, especially if each spouse has a profession that can be practiced only in a limited number of locales. Although a rare solution, there are couples in our society who do it. One well-known example is the case of Martha and Hicks Griffiths. During the week, if Congress is in session, she spends weekdays in Washington, D.C.; he remains in Detroit. On weekends, she commutes to Detroit; or occasionally, he commutes the other way.[7]

None of the professional couples opted for this solution on a long-term basis of many years. However, three couples, all with children, had divided the family and commuted for a definite period of time which was specified in advance. For example, one couple did this because the husband had a chance to further his education in another city. They knew when they decided to make the long commute that they would only have to do it for ten months.

Most couples resisted the idea of going to such extremes, especially as a long-term solution. But a few said they were willing to consider such an arrangement should the need arise.

Husband's View of the Wife's Travel

One might suppose that any husband would be upset about the prospect of his wife traveling alone on business. But on the contrary, most husbands in the professional couples were very supportive of their wives traveling without them and felt they should have this opportunity. Specifically, fourteen husbands took this view, accepting the travel as part of their wives having professions. They would have been embarrassed if their wives shirked their duties because of them.

Some of these couples accepted very easily both the idea of being apart from each other and the fact that during the wife's absence additional domestic responsibilities would fall on the husband. For example, one wife — a mother — described their separate travels as follows:

Oh we just accept it. We don't mind it. We're glad (laughter) to see each other again, but we just accept it as part of life. We don't ever have to be away very long, you see. If I go, it's perhaps a week or ten days. It's not a very long time.

And regarding her travel, the husband said:

Oh It think it's fine. I mean, the things she has to do in this field are very important. And as I say, you're restricted to using [equipment] in a few locations and so it's developed quite naturally [that she travels].

A few of these couples stressed the hardships involved, even though the husband did support the wife's travel. They found it hard to be separated, or the husband found it hard to cope with the domestic scene by himself. One such couple spoke as follows:

He accepts [my trips] but I don't think he likes them. . . . Part of the reason is because he's (laughter) stuck with the kids and that bothers him; he doesn't like it. And I don't like his going off either, so it's mutual.

(wife's interview)

Well the three days was nothing, but the month [she was away] I didn't like too much. . . . I mean it's just hard. . . . And the mail was fouled up. . . . and so I was quite angry because she didn't seem to be writing. . . . And taking care of the kids, I mean it's a tough job to take care of them all the time. . . . You have to be both parents to the kids, you have to take care of everything and at the same time carry on your own work. I mean that's just a tough job. [Do you feel that she perhaps should not go away on these kinds of trips?] No, no. It's just hard (laughter). I mean if I feel that she shouldn't go away, then I feel I shouldn't go away. And I think that sometimes you just have to do it. It's just part of the game.

(husband's interview)

There was considerable symmetry in the expectations of the four-teen couples described above, but in a few cases this symmetry did not exist. Here the wife reported that the husband's approval of her travels came only with many strings attached. There was a great difference in the attitudes toward her travel vs. those toward his travel. These few cases are in the minority in the professional group, but they raise important problems which women in our society face. They show one way in which women can get isolated from the mainstream of professional life, and they show how even in couples where the wife has a success-ful career, the expectations regarding husband and wife can still differ greatly.

One of these women, although she traveled a lot, seldom went to conventions. She saw that this resulted in a career deprivation for her, and she was beginning to feel the lack of contact. She did not attend for a variety of reasons. She saw conferences were an optional part of career performance. She was so busy traveling with her husband throughout the year that she really did not have the time. And also there was a marked asymmetry in the expectations of the couple regarding how free each one was to travel. She noted that one cannot just state simply that a husband objects or does not object to his wife's traveling. There are, she explained, so many degrees of objection. She described her husband's attitude and her own attitude as follows:

> *If I wanted to go to New York to see a play obviously my husband wouldn't say "I don't allow you to go." . . . He might say. . . . "If you go, please make arrangements fcr [our daughter] to get a ride to the party she's going to." These are all related to an internal family division of labor. That is, he says, "I have no objection in principle to your going provided you are responsible for the execution of your responsibilities in your absence." But you see, the going to conferences also comes under the same rubric.*

Regarding a three-month absence of hers, she described the complexities of her husband's attitude and concluded as follows:

> *The element of inequality when I made that analogy — that was quite deliberate when I said some men let their wives buy wardrobes as a dispensation, as a sign of their own success in life. Well the inequality that is implied in my husband's saying "yes, go" is of a different nature. It doesn't have that patronizing tone to it. But it's perfectly true that if the children had been small I could not have gone [on my three-month trip] because I cannot burden my husband with a time expenditure that his career will not permit.*

Her comments suggest that his time is seen as more valuable than hers, and that his career takes priority. The assumption is that she can afford to take time out for the children, but he cannot. This view was confirmed by the husband's interview. He explained that it had been clear for some time that his career was the principal one.

Another woman reported problems over her husband's attitude in connection with a three-week trip she wanted to make. She was contemplating going to Europe to attend a meeting. She wanted her husband to go too and thought they could then visit other places as well. But he felt uncomfortable being in a position in which he was accompanying her rather than vice versa.

> *He doesn't want to tail along behind me in a way in which I don't mind tailing along behind him. So he doesn't want to come along and doesn't know what he would do if he weren't tailing along behind me, which really means that I have to make up my mind whether I'm going to go alone or not.*

In addition to the issue of whether he would go, there were problems over who would care for the children in her absence.

The Traditional Couples

The traditional wives followed a pattern very different from that of the professional wives. Since their marriage, the traditional wives had not traveled alone on business. The only independent travel they had done was in connection with family responsibilities. For example, they had visited their own parents or grandparents, or they had been left behind to pick up a household and later join the husband at a new residence.

One reason, of course, for their lack of professional travel was that they had been away from their profession a number of years; but even in the few cases where the issue had arisen, the women did not feel free to travel. For example, one woman described an instance early in her marriage when she had wanted to travel but did not go:

> I suggested that I was going to go to [another city] to these meetings which were something like four days. And he was astounded! He said, "You know, you're not going to go and leave me, are you?" . . . [How did you feel about his expectation that you stay home?] Well, I was surprised. I think if I'd really thought about it I could have anticipated it. But, on the other hand, the desire to go was quite strong. (laughter) I don't know. That didn't sit well.

Much later in the interview, she described a very recent instance in which she could have made a professional trip, with expenses paid by the employing institution. But her description suggests that now she does not even bring up the matter for discussion with her husband; it has become almost unthinkable.

> I sort of said to myself, oh, that would be nice. And I immediately said, you know, that would be impossible. I couldn't really. I think that he would not go along with that.

In another traditional couple, the woman said she had been invited to go somewhere. She was sure her husband would encourage her to go. But she said, in practical terms, it was hard to see how she would be able to do it because she no longer had a housekeeper to look after the children.

Although the traditional wives stayed home, all their husbands traveled on business. Over half traveled "an excessive amount" — away from home on trips an average of two or three nights a week, off several summers alone, and covering as much as 100,000 miles in a year. Half the families had been separated geographically or done long-distance commuting for several months because of the husband's work. Thus the traditional couples did not escape the trials and tribulations of professional travel.

COUPLES CAN'T WORK HERE: ANTI-NEPOTISM RULES

Anti-nepotism rules are one more barrier to the two-career family, for they automatically reduce the number of jobs at one's disposal. These rules fall hardest on couples who actually want — or at least would be willing — to work at the same institution. They fall hardest on couples in which the husband and wife are in the same field; employers are particularly reluctant to have two related people in the same administrative section or department. These rules may be explicitly stated, or it may simply be understood that they will be applied on an informal basis. Six of the twenty professional couples had their jobs significantly affected by anti-nepotism rules. In five of these six couples the husband and wife were in the same field or in very closely related fields. Sometimes the difficulties were eventually overcome with both spouses getting full status in one department, and sometimes they were not.

Although anti-nepotism rules may be written without stating a sexual bias — merely saying that the employment of two related persons is forbidden — they are almost always applied against women. Indirectly they may affect the husband's career if he seeks employment only where his wife can work too; but once employment is obtained for one or both of them, if someone suffers, it is the wife who is made to suffer. Among the people interviewed, it was wives, not husbands, who were denied permanent employment, who were only permitted to officially work part time, who left if only one could be promoted.[8]

Two cases merit special discussion. Each is highly unusual among the couples interviewed, but each raises interesting issues relevant to how anti-nepotism rules affect the two-career family.

The first case is of interest because it illustrates how a wife's status may be very precarious. It shows a situation in which the woman had to rely on friendship ties to get things done because she lacked the rights that are associated with having a formal position. The husband and wife were in the humanities and were in the same field. Previously she was a tenured associate professor. Then the couple moved, and both became employed in the same college department. Although she wanted to work full time, she was permitted to work only slightly under full time — and no more. The university could thus deny her tenure on the grounds that she was not a full-time faculty member. She automatically lost several other rights: her salary declined; she was denied retirement privileges; and the question of a sabbatical, even a prorated sabbatical, was still up in the air. Equally important were the subtle changes that occurred. Little slights constantly reminded her of her precarious status:

> *[There are] little pinpricks which make me feel, or at least get a sense of how Negroes feel sometimes. Little things. Notices come around addressed to all full-time faculty. And I usually get them simply because the office girls know me and they consider me one of the department. Occasionally a new girl will come in and I won't get an important notice because she's simply reading it literally and it says to all full-time faculty. This kind of thing I find a bit difficult to live with. . . . I have established myself sufficiently at least on a kind of personal basis. I'm treated pretty much as a regular member, but it's tenuous because it is personal.*

A second specific case illustrates the behind-the-scenes manipulation that can occur to insure that formally the anti-nepotism rules are being met while informally they are being broken. In this case, both spouses were scientists. Frequently they worked together as a team. Both were well known and greatly in demand — a fact which no doubt increased employers' willingness to make exceptions for them. One university where they were employed did not permit two members of a family to be paid from the same budget, but this rule was circumvented because his salary came from university funds while hers was drawn from contract funds. The former, however, was a relatively stable source of money, but the contract budget fluctuated from year to year, thus putting the wife in a more tenuous position. Another university manipulated the rule against employing a husband and wife in the same department by listing the wife as formally affiliated with some other department, although in actuality she spent all her time in the same department with her husband. In this case, as in the case of the couple in the humanities, it is interesting that in manipulating the anti-nepotism rules it was the wife's position rather than the husband's that was adversely affected. She, not he, was paid with "soft money" and was given the "paper appointment."

THE ISOLATED AND THE UNAFFILIATED

The Unaffiliated

The fact that most professional work requires an institutional affiliation compounds the problems facing the two-career family. It is not only the working class that is alienated from the tools of production;

professionals are also alienated from the means of production.[9] Institutions, not private individuals, own the laboratories, the archives, and the computers, and, to a large extent, they control the flow of research funds. The unaffiliated have difficulty gaining access to these tools. They lose status, and they are more isolated from colleagues. Within a couple, if someone forgoes an appointment — because of anti-nepotism rules or for whatever reason — it is usually the wife.

Among the professional women interviewed, periods of attempting their regular work while having absolutely no formal affiliation were relatively rare.[10] When such periods occurred, there were difficulties. For example, one woman did research despite not being able to obtain a position. She said the laboratories did not make things very easy for her. They made her pay a fee for using the equipment. She did not feel very comfortable about the situation. Another woman spoke more of how she felt others perceived her because of being unaffiliated. Even though her articles had still been getting accepted for publication, the lack of affiliation — and the isolation — ebbed away her self-confidence.

> *Academicians are always a little bit skeptical and suspicious of somebody who doesn't have an affiliation with a university. . . . I had written a couple of articles which had been accepted. But the more time that elapsed in which I was away from the academic world, the more I wondered if it was worth submitting anything, because . . . I wondered whether they were going to say, "Oh, well, this is just an article from some woman, you know, who wants to fill in time."*

It was predicted that isolation would be primarily a problem among such unaffiliated women. But the interviews show that isolation can occur whether a woman does or does not have a formal affiliation.

The Isolated

Even when a woman follows the career route, there are a multitude of pressures which tend to isolate her from the mainstream of her profession. Women are apt to be removed from the various advantages and disadvantages which come from full participation in the colleague group; for example, access to new unpublished ideas, social support from the group, competitive pressure to keep up. The importance of colleague interaction has been shown in various studies. For example, recently an evaluation was made of the Radcliffe Institute's program to help women continue their careers. Women were asked about their experiences after receiving Institute fellowships. The evaluation showed that one of the most important parts of the program for the women was that it gave them access to stimulating colleagues. Appraisals and acceptance of their work by people whose opinions were relevant and respected increased their sense of professional identity.[11] This suggests that anything that limits opportunities for colleague interaction and increases isolation can be a career handicap.

Even though the women interviewed were very active professionally, some were adversely affected by isolation. Four of the twenty professional women in the present study were severely isolated when in graduate school or afterward. The case history of one such woman is presented in detail below. It is of particular interest for two reasons. First of all, it shows the great variety of factors which contribute to the isolation of women, especially married women, from professional life. Second, it shows both the advantages and disadvantages of working on the fringes of a profession. She began with her graduate school experiences:

The real crux of what it meant to be in graduate school while having a small child was that it meant that the kind of education that you get among peers, which is presumably one of the key things of the graduate education, I didn't have, except in a very restricted sense. And secondly, I could not commit myself to the kind of apprenticeship that people have. . . . So that I went through the two years of graduate school simply in the formal sense. . . . I did feel isolated partly because I couldn't sit around [and talk after class]. I went to class from home. I had a babysitter for a restricted number of hours because I couldn't afford more. And I came back from class when class was over. And I went to the library similarly on schedule. My husband and I took turns going to the library. So obviously I was isolated from whatever social life existed and from some of the contacts with faculty that you would get in this kind of apprenticeship clearly and this was very important for me. I'm feeling the effects of that lack in my work today.

After her exams, she was "turned loose somehow, somewhere, at some future date to do a dissertation." Her husband took a job elsewhere. She accompanied him. She had very tentative plans worked out for doing her research in that community. She began collecting data, but soon became interested in another very different topic. She felt the fact that she did not have the career obligations of a man made it easier for her to switch topics; here working on the fringes of the system proved to be advantageous.

I decided that, damn, that [research topic] was not what I wanted to work on. And I didn't think in terms of time on this. I didn't say, "Oh, my God, you know, I've got to get this grant renewed." I had no grant. Nobody was

*paying me for nothing. I was not dependent on anyone except [one pro-
fessor's] good will. My husband was supporting me. And I was meeting
all my research expenditures out of my own pocket. . . . I ended up writing
a thesis which contains — it's not yet published — but it contains material
about this community that nobody has ever — no outsider — has ever
found out or written about. . . . Why was I able to do that thesis? Simply
because I did not have the career obligations of a man. I didn't have to be
back because my sabbatical was going to run out. I didn't have to show
anybody that, "Yes, I'm a good boy, I have a publishable manuscript, you
can give me tenure." I didn't give a damn. I didn't even think about these
things.*

Several other factors contributed to this woman's isolation from
members of her own profession: The couple's moves had been primarily determined by the husband's career. She could not afford the
time to attend many conventions in her own field. She entertained a lot
for her husband's colleagues and spent more time with them than with
her own colleagues. She saw clearly the difference between doing creative work in isolation and doing it embedded in a full-fledged career.

*Those men who advise and say, "Oh, I only have 20 hours a week to spend
on my creative work and there is no woman who can't afford 20 hours a
week out of her housekeeping; therefore she ought also to be as creative
as I am." The man who says that doesn't know what he's talking about
because here you're talking about creativeness embedded in an ongoing
career as compared to creativeness for which the job has to be created. . . .
And that, if you ask me what I am resentful about, I'm resentful about
that attitude.*

As the above case shows, women are not isolated from the occupational world only by virtue of not being expected to have a serious
long-term career. Even if they do opt for a career, a multitude of factors
operate to isolate them from the mainstream of their profession. The
discussion of the etiquette in the male dominated professions, presented in a later chapter, gives further evidence of this.

CAREERISM AS AN ALL-CONSUMING ACTIVITY

Another barrier to two professions in the family is the present definition
of career as an all-consuming activity. The pressure that exists for
full-time work and uninterrupted careers is one of the many characteristics of occupations which are in keeping with this view. Preference is
given to the individual who works or studies full-time and who does

not take time off. Anything less than full-time employment may be difficult to obtain. Or, even if obtained, it may mean that one will be treated like a second-class citizen. Likewise, interruptions in employment may be looked upon with disdain: "gaps in the vita" are hard to explain away. This definition of career is especially a hardship for the family with two professions. It means that husband and wife each may be expected to pursue a life pattern so rigorous as to normally demand that the other spouse's interests be subordinated to it.

The Full-Time Uninterrupted Career — A Matter of Perception

To some degree, part-time status and career interruptions are matters of perception. In actual fact, employers and schools do make many special arrangements for part-time work and leaves of absence. The catch is that they only do it for individuals with socially acceptable reasons, and domestic responsibilities usually have not been one of these reasons.

Consider first the full-time/part-time issue. Often a man can get part-time employment — especially if the rest of his time is to be spent on another job. But often a woman cannot get part-time employment — especially if the rest of her time is to be spent with her family. Their requests for the part-time position are perceived differently by the employer. The person who splits the time between work and family is perceived as being less than professional.

The variability of what gets defined as full-time work has been analyzed by the well-known sociologist Everett Hughes. He says that full time is the amount of time which *men* ordinarily work, but that taking men as the norm somewhat begs the question. Nevertheless, one can measure full-time by a number of time units — hours of the day, days of the week, years of a life. Recently what is considered proper regarding all these measures has changed. He cites, as one example of change, that full time in the steel industry used to mean twelve hours per day, seven days per week. "The conception of full-time has remained constant only in referring to the standard amount of time given to work by men between school-leaving and retirement, defined in hours, days and years. The actual numbers in the equation vary."[12] He sees that full time, for many people, has been reduced in hours and days. If this goes much further, the "distinction between full-time and part-time will no longer refer to the number of hours and days, but simply to difference of rhythms, regularities and interruptions."[13]

Not only have social scientists commented on the inadequacies of these terms. A few of the professional women interviewed also did.

One stated:

> There are such things as jobs that are part time but full commitment and
> then there are jobs that are part time and part-time commitment. There's
> a very crucial difference. No writer is a part-time writer. You know, it's
> true that Kafka had a job during the day but would you call Kafka a part-
> time writer? You know, the word part time, when applied to commitment,
> is an indignity.

Sometimes the inadequacies of these terms made it necessary for the
woman to explain in which sense she was full time or part time. One
compared herself to her male colleagues as follows:

> I've never been full time, but I'll become full time. Though I think I give
> them full time, you know, in terms of the kind of attention I give the
> work. . . . So many of my colleagues I know spend so much of their time
> just doing nothing (laughter) or just sort of shooting the bull, which I
> don't have time to do so that I, you know, I almost give the same amount
> of time to it. But I call it part time.

Thus, when using these terms one must remember that they refer to
current definitions and that these may change.

Career interruptions are also partly a matter of perception.[14] There
is a difference between how different interruptions are defined. Men
often interrupt their careers for military service. Women often interrupt their careers for child rearing. For example, among the professional couples interviewed, half the women had interrupted careers —
usually because of child rearing. And half the men had interrupted
careers — typically for military duty. Thus half the women and half
the men spent time away from their professions — but for different
reasons. And these interruptions, at least up to now, have been perceived very differently by employers and educators. In a curious paradox of human values men have been criticized only slightly for career
interruptions in which their task was to kill off other members of the
human race; but women have been severely criticized for taking time
away from their profession in order to raise the next generation.[15]

Time Off A Privilege, Not A Right

There are several effects of the pressure for single-minded devotion
to a career. First of all, it means that any person who wishes to pursue
a profession less than full time has to make special arrangements to do
so. It is not an institutionalized pattern. Each person who wishes to do
this must make some kind of *ad hoc* arrangement and may even have

to fight for the privilege. For example, among the professional women interviewed, two who wanted to attend graduate school part time had to confront the administration over the issue. One explained how, contrary to her wishes, she was required to begin her studies with a full load. She said:

> *I did not want to do full-time studying and I went to the Dean and said, "Look, I've got a one-year-old at home. Can't I just take three courses and make it up during the summers?" And she was very dramatic about it and said, "No, if you're going to have a career you're going to have to show the men that you're twice as good as they are. But if you do well in your first semester then we will permit you to take a reduced program thereafter provided you take summer school work." And I was so angry at this that I think I had four straight A's that first semester. . . . but I worked like hell.*

Only after she "proved" herself was this woman granted the privilege of taking three courses a semester instead of the normal four.[16]

Even if one succeeds in making the special arrangements for part-time schooling or employment, one may not be thought of as a "real member" of the group. Schools and employers often make a big distinction between the way they treat full- and part-time personnel. People in the part-time category are often denied things such as the right to sit on decision-making committees, obtain a permanent position, or accrue fringe benefits.

The Rigorous Life Pattern of Career

A second effect of pressure for single-minded commitment to career is that it creates a very rigorous life pattern — a regimen to which other things must be subordinated. It creates, for example, a very hectic schedule in which time becomes a precious commodity — limited in supply and greatly in demand. This aspect is discussed later along with how couples budgeted their time and effort. Career, thus defined, takes a major portion of one's life.

The professional women interviewed are interesting in this connection. On the one hand, they devoted almost as much of their lives to career as men are expected to do. For example, looking at all twenty professional women combined, nine of them, including seven with children, had uninterrupted full-time careers. Among these nine some had never taken a leave of absence at all; none of them had taken more than a total of three months off in their entire career; and none had ever worked solely part time.

As another example, one can look at just those among the twenty who were mothers. These women tended to take a relatively small amount of time out for child rearing. For half the mothers the time out after childbirth was less than three months total, and when employed they always worked full time. The woman who took the least time off spoke as follows:

> *Oh well, you won't believe this. . . . I think two days is the maximum length of time I missed with any of the children. . . . A few of them were born over the week end. And only one was born during the week and I didn't even miss much with the one that was born during the week because it turned out there was a snow storm and [everything] (laughter) was closed that week, so I just missed two days on that one. I never missed more than that with any of them.*

Even those women who took several years off — one woman took five years off to raise her one and only child — still had a high rate of participation in the labor force relative to the traditional wives interviewed and certainly relative to the general female population. So in this sense, the professional women approximated the male model. The interviews support the conclusion of other studies which show that professional success among women correlates with a high level of participation in the labor force. Eli Ginzberg's study of women, for example, shows that a correlation exists between continuous work history and achievement, and he goes so far as to state that "a continuous work history is almost a prerequisite for high, or even good, achievement. A woman cannot reach the top in her field unless she is willing to devote a major portion of her life to work. Continuity is a necessary factor but not, of course, the only factor."[17]

On the other hand, a number of the professional women interviewed in the present study made departures from the patterns men typically follow. For example, almost half the professional women pursued their careers at some point, solely on a part-time basis. In contrast, hardly any of the men were ever just part time. Even more important, five of the twenty women achieved professional success via some very unusual career route — with success defined here either by formal job title or acclaim for published work. For example, one woman, who held the rank of full professor when interviewed, previously had been unemployed for five years and also had spent several years working only part time. In another case, there was a woman whose published work had been very favorably received by her colleagues, and yet her entire graduate school and employment experience so far had been done on a part-time basis. She fought for the privilege of attending graduate school part time, and said that if this had not been possible she would not have gone at all. She liked having, as she put it, the best of both worlds:

I enjoy working part time. . . . I don't think I'd enjoy a job where I just worked from 9 to 5 every day. I like this kind of [life]. I like doing my own work at the same time. . . . I think I have the best of both worlds. I hope my daughters find some way of combining marriage and a career. They plan to. I think it's great.

These five women dealt with the inflexibility of the occupational world in an innovative way. Their atypical career patterns resulted from *ad hoc* ways of coping with a rigid occupational structure. In this sense, the interviews support another very important conclusion: there are many different ways for a woman to succeed professionally. Many different career patterns can lead to success. This finding should be of great encouragement to women who either by circumstances have been unable, or by choice have not wished, to follow a more typically male career pattern. Indeed, it should be of encouragement to anyone — male or female — who wishes to challenge the current concept of career as an all-consuming activity.

NOTES

1. Hughes calls this the itinerant job market. See his distinction between two styles of careers, the home-guard and the itinerant. Everett Cherrington Hughes, *Men and Their Work* (Glencoe, Ill.: The Free Press, 1958), p. 129 and p. 136.

2. Talcott Parsons, "The Social Structure of the Family," *The Family: Its Function and Destiny*, ed. Ruth Nanda Anshen (New York: Harper, 1949), p. 192.

3. Philip E. Slater, "Some Social Consequences Of Temporary Systems," *The Temporary Society*, by Warren G. Bennis and Philip E. Slater (New York: Harper and Row, 1968), p. 91.

4. Elizabeth Bott, *Family and Social Network: Roles, Norms, and External Relationships in Ordinary Urban Families* (London: Tavistock Publications, 1957), p. 106 and p. 198; and Slater, *op. cit.*, pp. 88–90.

5. There have been studies of employers' attitudes and practices regarding employment of husband and wife at the same institution. See the discussion of some of these in Jessie Bernard, *Academic Women* (New York: World Publishing Co., 1966), pp. 102-03. (First published in 1964: Pennsylvania State Univ.)

6. Slater, *op. cit.*, p. 137; and G. P. Murdock, "Comparative Data on the Division of Labor by Sex," *Social Forces*, 15 (1937), pp. 551-53.

7. Their careers have been described in a recent book on women in politics. To commute cost them $5,200 in air fares in 1967. Peggy Lamson, *Few Are Chosen: American Women in Political Life Today* (Boston: Houghton Mifflin, 1968), pp. 90-91.

8. The kinds of difficulties which beset these couples are similar to the ones described in Rita James Simon, Shirley Merritt Clark, and Larry Tifft, "Of Nepotism, Marriage, and the Pursuit of an Academic Career," *Sociology of Education,* 39 (Fall, 1966), pp. 347-49.

9. See Weber's discussion on the concentration of the means of administration. He saw that concentration occurred in the research institutes of universities, too. "Through the concentration of such means in the hands of the privileged head of the institute, the mass of researchers and docents are separated from their 'means of production,' in the same way as capitalist enterprise has separated the workers from theirs." Max Weber, "Bureaucracy," *From Max Weber: Essays in Sociology* ed. and trans. H. H. Gerth and C. Wright Mills (New York: Oxford Univ., Galaxy Book, 1958), p. 224 (Trans. from *Wirtschaft und Gesellschaft,* Part III, Chap. 6, pp. 650-78.)

10. There were women who carried on professional work while having only a very tenuous connection to an institution; for example, while they were on leave of absence or after having moved far away. But even a tenuous connection gives one certain rights that one cannot have without an affiliation.

11. Martha S. White, "Psychological and Social Barriers to Women in Science," *Science,* 170 (Oct. 23, 1970), p. 413.

12. Everett C. Hughes, "Neo-Feminism: An Essay on Woman's Work," p. 3. (Mimeographed.)

13. *Ibid.,* p. 7. See also the discussion of Hughes' analysis by Riesman. David Riesman, "Introduction" in Bernard, *op. cit.,* p. xxiv.

14. In the present study, "career interruption" was defined as an interim period or periods totaling three months or more in which the person was neither a student nor an employee in the civilian labor force.

15. Motivationally, this is not a paradox. Killing and careerism are part of the same constellation. See, for example, Slater's analysis of male narcissism. Philip E. Slater, *The Glory of Hera: Greek Mythology and the Greek Family* (Boston: Beacon Press: 1968).

16. Some women suffer from the opposite problem. They want to work full-time but are forced into part-time status. See section on anti-nepotism rules.

17. Eli Ginzberg with associates. *Life Styles of Educated Women* (New York: Columbia University Press, 1966), p. 101.

5

Division of Labor: Stratification by Sex

> *I help because there is no other*
> *feasible way of running our men-*
> *age without a 24-hour-a-day house-*
> *hold staff.*
> Husband, professional couple

> *I feel it is the woman that keeps the*
> *house. . . . My job is to work on my*
> *studies. . . . The regular efficient*
> *running of the household I leave to*
> *her.*
> Husband, traditional couple

Our study of the two-career family could also be called a study in the division of labor by sex. So far, we have seen how the current expectations about family life and about occupations all have behind them the assumption that only one spouse will have a career. Yet, using our imaginations to do a kind of "thought experiment," we can see that the system could function whether the men held the occupational roles and the women the domestic ones, or vice versa. The one is but the mirror image of the other. The biological evidence does not seem to suggest any good reason for which way it should be. But in fact, as we all know, it is now the man who pursues a career and the woman who tends the home. Thus another way of stating the problem is to say that the one-career family represents a division of labor by sex, and that the two-career family challenges this distribution of activities.[1]

This sexual division of labor is also a stratification system based on sex. In other words, it is a form of social inequality by which the males are assigned the positions of prestige, while the females are excluded from them. Our society pays lip service to the virtues of parenthood, but in fact places a much higher value on occupational achievement. And it is the men who are assigned to the more prestigeful activities — career — and the women who are relegated to the less prestigious activities — family and home. This statement, of course, says nothing about whether the activities are satisfying or enjoyable, but only refers to one way that they are ranked in our society. The fact that motherhood can be a very satisfying experience does not make it any more prestigeful.

Social scientists seldom apply the concept "stratification" to the sexes, although they have applied it to almost every other form of social inequality. Apparently they do not perceive sex roles in these terms. William Goode, a sociologist known for his studies of the family, is somewhat of an exception. He has made analogies between women — the low-ranking sex — and people in other low-ranking categories. Looking at the division of labor in numerous societies, he notes that whatever the strictly male activities are, they are defined as being more honorific. This, he suggests, is similar to racial and caste restrictions. "The low-ranking race, caste, or sex is defined as not being *able* to do certain types of prestigious work, but it is also considered a violation of propriety if they do it. Obviously, if women really cannot do various kinds of male tasks, no moral or ethical prohibition would be necessary to keep them from it."[2]

Many social scientists, rather than questioning the existing stratification by sex, unwittingly provide a rationale to support it, thus suggesting that they themselves disdain some work as female. They frequently deprecate activities which are done by women and thus draw erroneous conclusions about what it is that differentiates between male and female activities. The best known and most influential of their theories is the instrumental-expressive one. It states that there is a difference between the roles of the sexes: Men have "instrumental" (task-oriented) roles and women have "socio-emotional" ones. The shortcomings of this view become apparent when one compares it with the facts of everyday life. For example, a man, even though he may only shuffle paper in a humdrum, bureaucratic, office job, is still said by this theory to be performing an instrumental role. But a housewife is said to have a socio-emotional role. She is not given credit for performing an instrumental role even though she may spend her day marketing, cleaning house, representing the family to outsiders (e.g., the pediatrician, the PTA), and fulfilling civic responsibilities. These social theorists do not see that a woman's day thus spent is task oriented and does involve a lot of hard labor. Ironically, by deprecating women's work in this way, these analysts fail to see what it is that really differentiates the roles of the sexes in our society. These social theorists typically maintain that the differential behavior of the sexes divides along instrumental-noninstrumental lines or along active-passive lines. A closer look suggests, however, that in many cases the real difference is between higher-status vs. lower-status tasks, or between more socially-valued vs. less socially-valued activities.[3]

Thus when women work in the professions they are challenging the existing division of labor — the existing stratification by sex. Two major questions arise: What happens in women's professional lives as they step into circles in which all the customs are based on a male fraternity? And what happens back home to their roles as hostess, as housekeeper, as mother, as server and promoter of the husband's career? These ramifications are explored below.

WOMEN IN THE MALE FRATERNITY

When women enter the male-dominated professions, the result is a contradiction of status. We ordinarily respond differently to a female than we do to a professional — and yet here we have both these characteristics combined in one individual. We ordinarily expect the person occupying a professional position to be a man, and when it is not we often do not know how to act.

It is this kind of problem that Everett Hughes has in mind when he says that certain peculiar combinations of status-determining characteristics make for contradictions and dilemmas of status. A set of auxiliary characteristics comes to be associated with a position, and then these auxiliary characteristics come to be expected of all the people who occupy that position. For many favored positions, the characteristics traditionally expected of incumbents have been white, Anglo-Saxon, male, and Protestant. Expectations about such auxiliary characteristics are enormously important in an occupation because they become part of the outlook of the established members of the occupation. "They become, in fact, the basis of the colleague-group's definition of its common interests, of its informal code, of selection of those who become the inner fraternity."[4] Thus, when new kinds of people — from a different race, or class, or sex — enter established positions, this produces a contradiction of status. And it not only creates a dilemma of status for the individual concerned, but also for the other people who interact with this person.

Even today the combined characteristics of female and professional can produce contradictions and dilemmas of status in a multitude of settings. Often the rules of the game — the etiquette, the mores — simply assume that the professional will be a man. If the professional is a woman, then there will be many occasions on which other people will not know whether to respond to her primarily as a professional or as a woman. A dilemma of this kind recently occurred in England when a woman judge was appointed to the High Court of Justice. A protocol crisis occurred over what the lawyers should call her. "My Lord" seemed confusing. But "Mrs. Justice" somehow did not sound right. Eventually it was decreed that for reasons of protocol, the lady should be referred to as a man.[5]

The professional women in the present study also reported a variety of examples of such contradictions. One woman reported that she was very good at climbing towers and walking out on beams like a steeple-jack; but she said, sometimes there are "stuffy old men" who do not like to see a woman doing such a thing. Another woman — in an industry-dominated and male-dominated field — said that meetings could be lonely. As a woman, she was hesitant to spend time socially with her male friends for fear they would not like it.

> *Many times when fellows go to conventions they like to go out to dinner and then perhaps to a girly show. . . . They hesitate if you're along and you don't like to cramp their style. So many times if I go to a convention it's a very lonely time unless I feel that I'm wanted in a particular group.*

In another couple, the wife was an accomplished and experienced scientist. But when the couple moved to a new institution, other people suddenly perceived her more as a woman. The method these other people used for dealing with the dilemma of status was to maintain the fiction that the wife assisted her husband in his work. Actually, the wife's work depended on access to very expensive equipment for gathering data. Everybody knew that she did the empirical work and that he was the theoretician. Yet everybody maintained the fiction that he was the one who used the equipment and she just went along to help him. When the work schedules came out saying who could use the equipment, his name — not hers — appeared on the list. Eventually the husband got together with a friend of his and raised a big fuss, saying that he and his wife would "no longer tolerate such antiquated rules."

> *She's one of the few women who've broken into this business you see. . . . There was a big battle kind of on her behalf which raged through [the organization] and brought in lots of prominent people because it was not realized [there] just how strong this prejudice was. We got to one point when the director . . . was reduced to saying, "Well it's not easy to have her there regularly because there's no ladies' room." You know, I mean this was kind of a last ditch stand.*

The husband told the story with great hilarity because in the end the couple finally won. It was formally acknowledged that she used and was entitled to use the equipment.

One last dilemma of status merits discussion. It arose because there were two careers in one family. The situation developed because of the very complex relationship which existed between the husband's career and the wife's career. In certain situations she acted as a professional in relation to her husband's colleagues. But in certain other situations, these colleagues, in effect, asked her to be a wife. At conferences, for example, she and the other professionally qualified wives were not allowed to be participants because there were so few of them. Their participation would have been socially awkward because the majority of men were not married to women of professional status. She described her feeling as follows:

> It is very rarely that I have to change hats but I sometimes do and then it is very painful. For there are circumstances in which my husband's job in effect demands that I be not involved, even though I could be. But, it would not be proper. It would offend other men whose wives do not have the same professional status I have. So in deference to these other men's feelings about their wives I have to step back and I don't like this one bit. I resent it very much because I think it is humanly unfair, but I do it.

The above examples were chosen not because they were typical or representative of all the professional women, but because they show a range of situations in which dilemmas of status can occur. Compared to many other societies and many other historical periods in which men and women literally live in separate worlds, the United States today — especially in the upper middle class — minimizes segregation by sex; but even in the United States there are a tremendous number of statuses for which there is a definite expectation concerning what sex the incumbent should be. So many forms of behavior — from climbing towers to paying the bill in a restaurant — are considered to be proper or improper, depending on the sex of the person. These expectations, even about seemingly minor forms of behavior, can affect male-female professional relationships. Female lawyers, in a recent study, mentioned again and again the difficulties involved in meeting a male colleague or client for lunch. There was always the "problem of the check at the end of the meal."[6]

These kinds of expectations can lead to a double bind situation. If the woman professional climbs the tower and pays the bill, she may be criticized for not being lady-like. But if she does the opposite, she may be criticized for not being professional.

THE PRETTY FLOWER BY HIS SIDE

Nothing could be more symbolic of the sexual division of labor in our society than the hostess role. There is an expectation that certain jobs will be held by men and that their wives will perform ancillary activities. The wife, although unpaid, is to perform duties which are an extension of the husband's job. Most typically these duties are associated with being a hostess and entertaining, and the wife may also be expected to attend certain functions or put in public appearances with her husband. The archetype of this feminine role is that of First Lady, but a similar phenomenon occurs when a woman's husband becomes a high-ranking military officer, a career diplomat, dean of a law school, a university president, or a corporation executive.[7]

This hostess role is symbolic of a division of labor in which women are to serve men. The man's total energies are to be used for the pursuit of his career. The woman is to make sure other tasks and activities do not distract him. He is expected to compete, be aggressive, and achieve success. She is expected to be the pretty flower by his side and add a note of charm and graciousness to the enterprise. The man is to do the higher-status tasks which we define as work. The woman is to do lower-status tasks like entertaining which we define as ancillary — a definition which obscures the fact that they too require a lot of hard labor. Many social theorists would probably see the hostess role — since it deals with social affairs — as supporting their idea that men have instrumental roles and women have socio-emotional ones. However, their analysis would obscure the fact that the hostess role also is instrumental, is task oriented, and requires hard — and worse yet, unpaid — labor. Cynthia Epstein is one sociologist who has stressed the hard labor involved in this ancillary role. Referring to the large-scale exploitation of middle-class wives at the sides of their husbands, she calls them "unpaid working women"[8]

Positions which require the spouse to entertain professionally are a barrier to the two-career family. If the husband holds such a job, the demands on the wife to perform ancillary functions for her husband may make inroads on the time and energy she can devote to her own work. If the job itself is held by a woman, then she has no wife to perform these social duties for her. Though there is in most cases some latitude in how much entertaining is required, one may still feel pressured to perform these duties.

The Professional Couples
Most of the professional women in the study solved the issue by de-

emphasizing the hostess role. They gave only a minimum of professional parties. Some couples had a policy of not attending social affairs at each other's place of employment. For example, one woman, when speaking about whether there were social obligations because of her husband's job as a professor, said she was not a faculty wife at her husband's institution. She had given some parties the year before when her husband was chairman of his department, but in general she did not feel any obligation to invite everybody to parties. She also said they kept socials at each other's institution to a minimum. If she was free to accompany her husband, then she went; but otherwise, she just sent her regrets.

Only three of the twenty wives fulfilled the job-related hostess role to any great extent. These three did it with varying degrees of enthusiasm. One stressed how much huge dinner and cocktail parties exhausted her. She talked of how it took so much out of her to get both her career and other responsibilities done:

> To do these things and satisfy my conscience that I'm not neglecting him, that I'm not neglecting even the fact that I am a faculty wife. There are people who must be invited and all that kind of thing — visitors in town. I go to great pains to do these things properly. I think the only thing we both regret about it is that it wears me out a great deal. It is a little too much. I need more time.

In contrast, the woman who entertained the most greatly enjoyed it. She took great pride in her style of entertainment, paying a great deal of attention to who she invited, what she served them, how she seated them. She kept a very careful record book of this, partly for tax purposes but partly to keep a record of who had eaten what at her house and who had come when. The husband explained in his interview that all his recent jobs had required entertainment. He elaborated as follows:

> All of my jobs . . . have required entertainment. . . . We take it very seriously. We make up lists of people we think would be interesting, get along well together. Of course we always do it jointly, with my wife doing most of the work, though, I'm afraid.

On the whole, the wife was enthusiastic about it. She said, "This is a nice part of my husband's job that I have and I like it."

Two of the twenty women themselves had held jobs requiring entertainment. They were too busy to do the preparation themselves and, of course, did not have wives to do it for them. These women solved the problem by doing their professional entertaining in restaurants. This is a solution which saves time but which may cost more money.

The Traditional Couples

The traditional wives were more likely to elaborate the hostess role than the professional wives were. In general, they reported this in positive terms. One professor's wife spoke as follows:

> We do a lot of entertaining. I had breakfast company this morning — a man who had a proposal that he wanted to put in my husband's hands. . . . It's not unusual for me to have dinner company, say, twice a week. . . . I'm a pretty well organized hostess and I enjoy it. . . . I can't say that there haven't been times when I haven't felt under considerable pressure, but on the whole I don't [feel under pressure]. And I do enjoy having these people come. Even though you might call it business entertaining, it's usually people that I'm interested in meeting and enjoy talking to and listening to. It's not a phase of [my husband's] job that I dislike. I like it.

The husband told of how he simply took it for granted that she would entertain for him.

> We do a lot of entertaining. I expect her to. I mean I bring home people at the drop of a hat. [Is this important to your work?] I think it's an important part. I know some people don't take it as being that. I think it is — entertaining students or entertaining faculty friends. . . . I would say that probably 15 or 20 times a year we'll have a little party or little gathering. I expect her to do it. And she does it. She's always done it.

In another couple, the woman reported that she did not return to work because her husband felt that she would have enough to do simply as the wife of a person in his position. She entertained a constant stream of visitors, colleagues, and students for him. She enjoyed doing it, and it was really what occupied her full time. Asked whether she felt burdened by this, she said, "Not really, because I considered this my function in life."

THE POLITICS OF HOUSEWORK

The current sexual division of labor seen so vividly in the hostess role also appears in the realm of routine housework. Again, women are to serve men. The husband is to devote himself single-mindedly to the pursuit of a career. The wife is to help by being the housekeeper and thus freeing him from distracting, lower-status domestic duties. The question is what happens when the wife follows a serious career. Does she accept outside employment and yet still retain most of the domestic duties? Or is her involvement in the outside world paralleled by a change in the division of labor within the home? It is this issue that has led the new feminists to talk about the "politics of housework."[9]

Amount of Work Done by Each Spouse

From the point of view of having time and energy for one's profession, the amount of housework done by each spouse seems more relevant than which specific tasks each person does. Thus the household division of labor is first discussed from this point of view.

The professional wives were by no means completely responsible for performing all the household tasks themselves. Their burden was lessened in two ways — by hired help or by assistance from the husband. First of all, almost all the professional couples interviewed employed domestic help on a regular basis. Usually they employed one person; however, in five cases the couples employed two people — one woman for child care and another, usually one day per week, for house cleaning. Only three couples had no hired domestic help when interviewed. For two of these, the reason was simply that they had become discouraged over the performance of prior domestics, and they decided that it was easier if they just split up the work among themselves. Strictly speaking, the delegation of work around the home to employees — although it represented a change in the husband and wife roles — did not represent a change in the sexual division of labor. Hired work was done by a person of the same sex to which the task traditionally belonged.

The second solution was that many professional wives received assistance from their husbands in the house. For example, couples were asked how these housekeeping tasks got done: Grocery shopping, cooking breakfast, cooking dinner, washing dishes, emptying the garbage, doing the laundry, ironing, vacuuming, and other cleaning. And in slightly over a third of the couples, the husband helped regularly with a number of these tasks.[10]

We have asked if the wife ends up with two jobs. We should ask the same of the husband. Must he do his professional work plus all the household repairs and heavy yard work? Just as much of the housework was delegated to someone else, the same was true for repairs and yard work. In most professional couples, a considerable portion of these tasks was done by hired help or by the wife.

Who Does What

Besides the issue of how much total housework each spouse does, it is also of interest to ask which specific tasks each person does. This question sheds light on the degree to which sex roles are seen as stereotyped. Are there certain tasks that only husbands or only wives do? Are tasks switched back and forth? Why are tasks assigned to a particular person?

First of all, trends did occur in who did specific housekeeping activities. For example, the tasks most likely to be done by the wife were cooking dinner and grocery shopping, and those most likely to be done by the husband were emptying garbage and trash, repair work, and heavy yard work. Tasks most likely to be shared equally between husband and wife were cooking breakfast and washing dishes. Financial tasks tended to be randomly allocated; for example, keeping track of the money and paying monthly bills were two tasks as likely to be assigned to one spouse as the other. Tasks most likely to be hired out were ironing, vacuuming, and general cleaning.

Secondly, although the tendency was to assign a task to a particular person, there was a lot of interchangeability. If the person who typically did it could not — for example, was out of town or was busy — then someone else would take over. And since in these small isolated families few people are available to pinch hit, this means that tasks typically performed by the man are done by the woman, and vice versa.[11]

Thirdly, in giving reasons for the allocation of specific tasks, the professional couples seldom cited ideological justification. They hardly ever said "that's man's work" or "that's woman's work." A few described their present division of labor in terms of whether it was "fair," saying that it was important to share the load. But, rather than ideological reasons, the couples gave pragmatic reasons for allocating specific tasks. One major reason given for why a person did a task was availability — that is, a combination of having time, being where the task was to be done (e.g., being at home, driving past the grocery store anyway, being employed near an auto repair shop), and fitting the task into the family schedule. For example, in one family it was the husband who took the baby sitter home at the end of the work day because that way the wife could start cooking dinner. In another example, the wife had cooked the breakfast while they were in graduate school, but when she began to teach the schedule changed, and the husband took over.

I had to take a 7:30 train which meant that unless I wanted to get up at the crack of dawn, it would be rather difficult. So my husband said, "Why don't I get breakfast." He had, I think, classes which started at 10:00 and . . . was 10 minutes walk from [the campus].

A second reason for allocation of specific tasks was skill. For example, in one couple, the wife did all the driving, even on vacations, because the husband did not know how to drive a car. In another couple, the husband and wife shared the preparation of dinner because they were both good cooks. A third reason was interest vs. apathy about whether the task got done. One woman explained how she simply did not care about the yard.

> *He does that out of my complete apathy. . . . Sometimes I mow the grass. I always mow the grass if he's not here when it's due to be mowed. . . . But I don't dig any dandelions out of the lawn because I don't care. They can grow as far as I'm concerned.*

A fourth reason was enjoyment or dislike of doing the task. For example, some women loved to cook and made special dishes as a hobby. In another couple the woman absolutely hated vacuuming, but her husband did not mind doing it.[12]

Feelings about the Division of Labor

Most of the professional women gave relatively positive replies concerning how they felt about the present division of labor. Specifically, two thirds expressed this view. Their replies typically emphasized the importance of family members pitching in and helping each other out, or they stressed how grateful they were because their husbands were such a tremendous help to them around the home. For example, one woman, describing how helpful her husband was with the housekeeping, concluded as follows:

> *We share evenly, and I think this is one of the important things if a woman is going to be active professionally that she have a husband who is considerate and helpful.*

The other third of the women gave somewhat more problematic replies concerning how they felt about the division of labor. Most commonly, these women felt resentful over having so much to do. However, they added either that the husband probably felt the same way about his tasks, or that the solution was not to burden their husbands. For example, one woman said:

> *I resent having to do it, but I don't feel that I want him to do it. I just cannot find a happy arrangement. I often feel pressed for time, and so I don't like having to do it. . . . On the other hand, my resentment isn't taken out on him because I don't think that he should do it. I might have felt very differently if I'd married a young man and I were in my twenties. . . . I think I might have felt differently, if I'd been much younger, about a man's sharing more of the work.*

The husbands were asked how they felt about the division of labor. Almost all the husbands in these professional couples helped around the home one way or another — either when interviewed or in the past. Asked why they were willing to do so, the most common reason given was that it seemed to be a physical necessity or that it was the only feasible way of getting things done. As one explained:

There is no other feasible way of running our menage without a 24-hour-a-day household staff which, so far, we can neither afford nor desire.

Although some felt it was a burden, or at least time-consuming, to help around the home, it still seemed worthwhile to do it so the wife could continue her work.

Several husbands said they enjoyed doing things around the home or that they had just fallen into the pattern without giving it much thought. A few stressed how easy it was to help out because of all the modern appliances. A few stressed the idea of sharing; having a family meant doing things for one another.

Coping with the House

Shifting the housework from the wife to someone else is not the only way of managing the home when both spouses work. People, in describing their division of labor, mentioned a variety of other techniques they used for coping with the house. Most of these fall into three categories: Increasing efficiency, lowering standards, or using money to save one's own time and effort.[13]

First of all, many couples reported increasing the efficiency of housework through the use of machines. Comments in the interviews indicate they owned numerous appliances. For example, even though they were not asked about what machines they owned, fourteen of the twenty couples mentioned that they owned dishwashers. And a number also mentioned owning other appliances such as washer-dryers. A family with two professional incomes can afford such a solution, whereas a family with a working wife at a lower economic level might not be able to.

Spouses in two thirds of the couples described other techniques they used for increasing the efficiency of housekeeping and for streamlining or eliminating certain tasks. For example, several women did a lot of the cooking ahead of time, perhaps on the week end. Several people deliberately minimized ironing by buying only easy-care clothing. And two couples, when having houses built, deliberately had them designed for efficiency of housekeeping specifically because the wife worked.

Secondly, eight professional women raised the issue of whether or not they could tolerate relatively low standards of housekeeping. Half of these very easily accepted some untidiness in the house. In describing the organization of her time, one said:

You must begin with what one does not do. I have a cleaning woman . . .

and what she doesn't do, doesn't get done. My kitchen shelves are cruddy,
but it doesn't bother me. Dust sits around. It doesn't bother me that every-
thing isn't shipshape. . . . The way a house is kept is not the most important
thing in the universe.

The other half of these women reported some difficulty in "looking
the other way" when household affairs were not perfect. For example,
one said:

I think this is my own fault. I think I like to make my own decisions about
these things. There are days when I feel I'd eat anything anyone put in
front of me as long as I didn't have to think about it. But when it comes
down to brass tacks, I wouldn't like to . . . be at the mercy of anybody
else. . . . I tend to be — everybody says so, so it must be true — a bit of a
perfectionist. . . . This is one of my problems — not wanting to do it, but
not being satisfied with the way somebody else does it.

This woman applied the "bit-of-perfectionist" standards to the office
too. Her desk was almost geometrically neat when she was interviewed; yet she described it as messy and said it bothered her that it
was untidy. She could neither compromise easily nor get everything
done herself with ease. This caused her considerable difficulty in trying to combine marriage and career.

Thirdly, a very important technique was the professional couples'
willingness to use money to save their own time and effort. This will
be discussed more in the chapter on the allocation of family resources.

The Traditional Couples
Both in attitude and deed, the traditional couples retained a greater
split between housekeeping as the wife's domain and career as the husband's domain. The traditional wives did housekeeping tasks themselves more than the professional wives did. They were less likely to
delegate tasks to hired help. And they received much less assistance
from their husbands; for example, traditional husbands hardly ever
did any of the nine housekeeping tasks previously discussed.[14]

As for attitudes, most traditional wives said things such as it was
not right to expect the husband to do housework in addition to his
own work, or that the husband expected to have these things done for
him. One woman explained how she felt about the division of labor
as follows:

I've always reckoned that he needs all the time that he has at home for his
work. I know that he's brilliant. . . . I feel that I just haven't got a right to
insist on using that time which is really valuable to him and valuable to
people beyond him for doing tasks which don't contribute anything in a

way. When they have to be done, well, I do them. I try not to fuss about having to do them.

Most traditional husbands expressed negative attitudes about helping with housekeeping tasks. They either said the house was the wife's responsibility, they disliked doing domestic tasks, or that they had too much else to do. One man explained.

I feel it is the woman that keeps the house. This is her area of sovereignty to a certain extent. This must sound terrible — 17th century! (laughter) There's nothing that I wouldn't do if there was a crises. But as a regular practice my job is to work on my studies. . . . The regular efficient running of the household I leave to her.

Another man said frankly, and with no apologies, that he thought his wife should run the house and also write out all the checks; he said he could put his time more profitably to other things.

CHILD REARING IN ISOLATION

The sexual division of labor appears again in child rearing. Here, however, the division of labor issue is enormously compounded by the isolation of our small family units. In the isolated nuclear family the husband and wife are the only two adults, and thus they alone are literally responsible for *all* the tasks involved in earning a living and running a home. They must be self-sufficient on a day-to-day basis in many ways which would not be necessary if the family was embedded in a larger extended family or in a more communal setting. Although many kinds of family help can be extended across vast distances, this is difficult to do for the everyday tasks of running the home.[15]

The isolation of the family constitutes a major barrier to the two-career family because of the enormous difficulties it poses for child rearing. Machines and outside services such as laundries can minimize the housekeeping, but the child-care problem in the isolated family is not so easily solved. The place of work is separate from the family's place of residence, so one spouse must leave the home to hold a job. Since most families do not have ready access to assistance from other adult relatives, servants, or child-care centers, one spouse typically must remain at home to care for the children when they are young. It is now the woman who does this.

The isolation of the family also creates a kind of double bind for the woman. If she stays at home to look after the children, she is deprived of a profession and the contacts with other people that a profession brings. But if she works, there is no one to look after the children. Philip Slater comments as follows on how this isolation creates awkwardness in the female role:

> One has only to see a village community in which women work and socialize in groups with children playing nearby, also in groups, supervised by the older ones, or by some of the mothers on a haphazardly shared basis, to realize what is awkward about the domestic role in America. Because the American mother is isolated, she can engage in only one of these three activities at a time — with effort, two. Even taken together they hardly constitute a satisfying occupation for a civilized woman.[16]

He notes also the shortcomings in the design of the modern suburban home. "The idea of imprisoning each woman alone in a small, self-contained, and architecturally isolating dwelling is a modern invention."[17]

There are at present no collective solutions to the problems that isolated families face in finding child care. We no longer share child care informally as in a small village community, and we have not yet widely and effectively established community-sponsored nurseries which would be a modern counterpart. If both spouses wish to remain in the labor force while their children are young, the couple must come up with their own *ad hoc* solution. They must make individual privately-financed arrangements for the day-time care of their children. Or they must make some modification in their own work routine.

The professional couples interviewed solved the problem of child care mainly in three ways: the husband routinely helped his wife with the children; the wife modified her work schedule; or the couple hired help.

Husband's Participation in Child Rearing

One way to cope with child care in the two-career family is for the husband to help. In most professional couples with children, the husband gave his wife considerable assistance with the routine aspects of child care. The men helped with tasks such as changing diapers, feeding children, putting them to bed, getting up at night with a crying child, or general looking after the children. To be precise, in twelve of the sixteen couples with children, the husband helped with child rearing on quite a regular basis. And this was so according to both the report of the wife and the report of the husband. For example, one husband described his involvement as follows:

> *I've done a lot of looking after the children. I'm an old hand at diapers. . . . We both had jobs — a job you could leave in a crisis. For example, if*

a child got the flu, I could take off. I do teaching and research; I can take time off. . . . We're wrapped up with our three children. I play baseball with them . . . or take the children to museums and shows. I watch children's TV shows with them — that's what they wanted me to do.

Several husbands had done a lot of baby sitting even during the day. Some found this a very easy arrangement. Some, as the following quote shows, found it a burden — although a worthwhile one.

I stayed on for a second year . . . so that she could finish her course work. Now this did create some problems in terms of taking care of our son. . . . I did a lot of baby sitting which was possible for me to do because I was writing my thesis. I didn't have any office hours. I could do a lot of the work at home. . . . We couldn't afford much help. [Did this become a burden for you?] Yes, it was a burden, but it seemed worthwhile, so that she could get her degree.

Flexible work schedules make it possible for couples to care for children in this way. Two couples found this such a satisfactory arrangement that they did it for a period of several years. In these two cases, the husband and wife arranged their schedules so that one or the other of them was always home during the day; thus, they never had to hire help for child care. These cases are interesting because they show how the issues of the two-career family can affect not only the wife but also the husband.

There were also other ways that some of the husbands helped with the children. For example, they shared the driving connected with having children. Or they assumed an additional amount of child-rearing responsibilities when the wife was away on trips. In one of the more extreme cases, the wife was gone several months. The husband, along with hired help, cared for their pre-school children during her absence.

Modified Work Schedules

A second technique used to cope with child care in the two-career family was to modify work schedules. Some people, as previously discussed, juggled routines informally. But in addition, others made this an official arrangement. There was a division of labor in this regard among the couples interviewed. If someone made an official modification, it was typically the wife rather than the husband who did so. Half the women, at some point in their careers, made special arrangements with their employer or school regarding time schedules because of family responsibilities. They either worked less than full time, or they made special arrangements about which particular hours they would work. For example, one woman who worked full time, as measured in number of hours, arrived at work each day forty-five minutes later than was normally required. This arrangement made it easier to take care of the children in the early morning. A few husbands, whose jobs — even without making special arrangements with the employer — gave them considerable control over their own time, also modified their schedules. But this was not official. They simply planned their day so as to be at home when the wife had to be away.

It was, incidentally, child rearing far more than childbearing that posed difficulties for the women's careers. For example, most women who took leaves of absence or modified their work schedules, did so primarily to rear their children, not to bear them; indeed, most of the women worked during pregnancy. The distinction between these two activities is important for the following reason. Though pregnancy and child bearing attest to a biological difference between the sexes, child rearing has been socially allocated to women and is thus more amenable to change. It is thus important to emphasize that the biological division of labor was much less of a career handicap for women than was the socially defined division of labor between the sexes.

Hired Help

The third technique for coping with child care in the two-career family was to hire help. Most professional couples with children did employ such help to assist them when the children were young. Specifically, thirteen of the sixteen did so. The arrangements varied from full-time live-in help to day-time baby sitters who came a certain number of hours per day and days per week.

Only a few professional couples had been able to raise children while employing little or no help. In these few cases, the wife was unemployed a few years, the husband and wife arranged their daily schedules so that if one was gone the other was home, or the grandmother did a lot of baby-sitting. The isolation of the family is illustrated by the fact that in only two cases were the wives' mothers able to help them on a regular basis. In most couples, the wife's mother lived in a different city, was dead or very elderly, or was off having a career of her own.

Hiring help involves, first of all, finding someone suitable to hire. The criteria that couples most often used for judging sitters were "reliability," "good with kids," and "an ability to handle the situation." The first criterion, reliability, meant several things. Very basically, it meant that the person showed up on the job when she said she would. The importance of this is shown in the following quote from a woman whose prior sitter was not reliable. She said:

I used to be in a panic every morning — is she going to come or isn't she going to come. And then there would be the inevitable phone calls, "My car broke down," "I'm sick," this, that, or the other thing. . . . Having somebody living in certainly is more peaceful in that respect. That made a lot of difference because I used to agonize every morning about whether I was going to make it (laughter) to where I was going.

This professional woman is the one who had the most trouble getting reliable help for child care. She added, "It's a grind to have to think about it all the time." Couples also wanted help they considered reliable in the sense of being trustworthy, responsible, and being someone with whom one could feel secure about leaving a child.

The second criterion, "good with kids," meant that the sitter was someone who enjoyed children. The kids liked her, and she took an interest in them above and beyond the money involved. The ultimate test was whether the children seemed happy or upset. Parents either observed their child's reactions to the sitter, or listened to what the child said about the sitter. For example, one of the men who reported favorably on the care given by sitters, spoke as follows about how he judged them.

Well by the criterion that [our daughter] was well and happy. She seemed to react very well to them and we reacted very well to them. They seemed to take a great interest in her over and above the financial aspects of the whole thing.

The third criterion, "an ability to handle the situation," meant the sitter knew what to do. She was experienced in caring for children and she could cope with whatever situation arose. As one woman said, you need somebody who is "unflappable." She later elaborated, saying "you try like the dickens to get somebody who could carry on if she got into trouble." She said, for example, you need a sitter who could decide on her own whether to go ahead and call a doctor.

One man's comments are of interest because he so strongly emphasized that having a competent sitter was *the* crux of the couple's situation. Speaking of their long-time sitter he said:

The nurse is the crux of our situation, so I might give you a line on her. We soon found she was extremely pleasant and competent. She is warm. She is a marvelous cook and marvelous with children. . . . Never any significant problems with [the children] so far, knock on wood. This has left my wife with a clear field. The children were always very well looked after under the care of this nurse. She can cope with anything. She's coped very splendidly. She knows about colds, etc. Both of us can feel the kids are looked after as well as if we were there — I can honestly say that.

It is not necessary to have a mother present all day long, as long as they get enough time with the parents.

The point he makes about the nurse as the crux of the situation cannot be overemphasized. With few other ways to care for children in the parents' absence, finding competent help becomes all important. Almost all the couples who had hired sitters in general had been satisfied with the care given their children. But in some couples there had been intermittent periods when the particular sitter they had was unsatisfactory. This was very painful to them. They found it very hard to fulfill their professional commitments when it meant leaving their children in the hands of someone of whom they disapproved.

Finding someone acceptable to employ is only one step in making satisfactory arrangements for child care. Another equally important step is that the parents, especially the mother, have to be willing to relinquish their exclusive control over child care. This refers to control both over the performance of certain tasks and over the emotional attachments developed by the child. It requires an ability to watch hired help do certain tasks differently from the way one would do them oneself. The woman in the following quote, for example, tells how she tried, in general, to let the sitter carry on in her own style:

> *She has very definite ideas on things. And, well, in a few cases I have asserted myself, in cases such as the matter of toilet training. . . . But I try not to direct too much unless it's something I feel very strongly about. And I have found that the children themselves, over the years, are very willing to accept different points of view from their parents and from the babysitter.*

In addition, it also may mean not objecting if the child develops some positive emotional attachment to the sitter. For example, one woman commented:

> *When it came time to hire someone after my little boy was born I found a lady who seems absolutely ideal. . . . The children adore her, she adores them, and I just couldn't feel better about it.*

It was clear that this woman did not feel threatened by the relationship that existed between her children and the sitter; instead she saw it in positive terms.

Child-Rearing Ideology

A complex ideology has traditionally supported the sexual division of labor for child rearing that exists in our society. The ideology includes the idea that women should serve men by making sure that distracting things, like child rearing, do not interfere with the men's work. But even more important, the ideology places tremendous emphasis on the need for the mother's full-time presence in the home for the sake of the child. Both academic and popular writers have expounded this view. They have written articles on the dangers of maternal deprivation, and they have emphasized the dangers of the working mother. Dr. Spock's record-selling book on baby care is one of the most famous examples, for his position is quite clear that a woman's place is in the home. Mothering is such a crucial task, he claims, that it requires full-time attention; anything less may result in a child that is a social problem. Spock retains this view even in his recent 1968 edition: "If a mother realizes clearly how vital this kind of care is to a small child, it may make it easier for her to decide that the extra money she might earn, or the satisfaction she might receive from an outside job, is not so important after all."[18]

This view recently has come under attack. Many academic and popular writers now focus on the problems of the mother's over-involvement and the father's lack of involvement in the socialization process. However, the older ideology has by no means completely disappeared. And it certainly was prevalent when the couples interviewed began raising their families. It posed a barrier for women. The older ideology might not have been grounded in factual evidence. But it nevertheless meant a woman had a career only in the face of dire predictions from others about what it would do to the children. In this respect it is of interest to see how far the professional couples' own views deviated from the ideology prevalent at the time.

Most of the professional women with children expressed very positive views about having someone else look after their children for at least part of the time.[19] Twelve of the sixteen who were mothers felt that it is good for the mother, for the child, or for both, if someone else does part of the rearing. They frequently said that they themselves would not be able to tolerate caring for young children on a full-time basis. Left at home for the full-time care of youngsters they would feel frustrated and inhibited. They would not be relaxed with the children and would push the children too hard. After speaking favorably of having other people care for children, one commented:

I suppose I feel this way because I myself don't feel qualified to cope with little ones all day long as a full-time proposition. It would drive me crazy. Therefore, the people who do, must be better (laughter) than I am.

They also frequently said it was better for the child's sake that the care not be given exclusively by the mother because having someone else for part of the time made the child more independent and self-reliant. They felt that it was good to expose children to other people with other points of view and that it was good not to have such a strong single tie between mother and child. As one said:

> *Also I feel that children are better off the more different people they associate with. I think that a child who grows up only with mother has an awfully narrow outlook on life. And when mother does go away, it's just traumatic.*

A few women gave a more qualified answer. Although they had had hired help or shared a lot of responsibilities with the husband, they had taken time off from work "to enjoy the child" or had done a lot of their work at home so as "to be available." Only one woman felt that the ideal situation was that the mother always do the care herself. She left her children with a sitter, and she felt she over-compensated to make up for this. She said, "I think I'm knocking myself out with this 'togetherness.' I think it's just over-compensation."

Although willing to have others care for their children part of the time, a number of women wanted to have the freedom to spend considerable time with the children when they were young. Several who had been able to take a year or so off, work part time, or follow a flexible time schedule when the children were young, expressed great satisfaction over this fact. One said:

> *I loved being a full-time mother and this was one of the greatest delights of my life. . . . For me this was a real great solid thing of enormous psychological significance. . . . I was damned glad that I didn't have the kind of career where, my God, if I'm absent for three months everything falls apart. I was absent for a year, you know, and that was just fine.*

But time off is not always easy to arrange, and this is one way in which the rigidity of the occupational system works a hardship on people.

As for husbands among the professional couples, half expressed favorable attitudes toward having someone other than the mother look after the children part of the time. They said it was not necessary to have a mother there all day as long as the children got enough time with the parents. They did not believe the old shibboleths about child-rearing and felt that it was good for the child to have diverse associations. If the mother stayed home all the time she would become frustrated.

A few husbands, although supporting the wife's career, qualified their answers more. They did not want the wife to have a full-time job when the children were young; or they thought the husband and wife should alternate schedules so one parent would always be home. A few husbands had neutral replies; they did not think it made much difference one way or the other.

The Traditional Couples

Both in practice and attitude, the traditional couples placed a greater emphasis on child rearing as the wife's domain. The traditional wives, relative to the professional wives, received less assistance from the husband in child-rearing tasks; they delegated less to hired help. For example, most traditional husbands participated only very occasionally in daily routine child-rearing tasks such as changing diapers or putting a child to bed. Their time with the children was more apt to be spent doing leisure activities, talking, or involving the children in something they had to do such as yard work. Most traditional husbands did spend time with their children in these kinds of activities. Only two of the seven traditional couples had hired sitters on a regular long-term basis over a period of several years. In two other cases, the couple had tried such an arrangement, but only briefly — perhaps for a year.

The traditional wives, relative to the professional wives, placed greater emphasis on the need for the mother's presence at home. Only one of the seven found it easy to delegate routine child care to a regular baby sitter. The others wanted to care for the children themselves. Of these, some wanted to do the daily care, but they did so without becoming overly possessive. They enjoyed doing it. But, as the children grew older, they began to look about for other activities to occupy their time. One of these commented:

> I personally would prefer to take care of them myself. I don't feel strongly on principle that any woman who doesn't is neglecting her duty. . . . But personally I prefer doing it myself. . . . I would not have considered in their preschool years leaving them on a regular schedule to be brought up by someone else.

Two traditional wives, however, were extremely possessive of their children. For example, one of these women worried about how adequate she was at mothering. She believed that a child needed a one-to-one relationship and thought it was very naughty for a woman to return to work while her child was still a baby. She absolutely worshiped her first child. She said, "I adored him until he was eighteen months old." But as he began to get more active, she said she felt rejected by him; she found it very painful when he showed signs of independence and did not need her as much. The other such woman found it difficult to delegate any work that she could do faster herself, and she could not give up her exclusive control over the child. She had tried sitters for a year, but it did not work out.

> *I had very much wanted to have a child and the fact that it was difficult to bear the child added to the adoration. This was going to be someone I was really going to be able to bring up. The influence [one has] on students is more tenuous. . . . [The sitter] was going to go on with her fantasy of bringing up my child. When [he] was two and a half, she was no longer intellectually adequate for him. She could no longer answer his questions. . . . I decided not to take the job [that I was offered]. I eased her out of the house.*

The extreme degree of possessiveness over a child, which these two women felt, never occurred among the professional women who were mothers.

The views of traditional husbands on child rearing did not fall into any typical pattern. At one extreme, there was the attitude that the only justifiable reason for a mother to work was that of economic necessity. At the other extreme, one man expressed the attitude that his spouse could not get away from his son, and, in his opinion, everybody would be better off if she would get out of the house.

SERVER AND SERVED

A way of summarizing the issues of this chapter is to look at who is served and who serves. This division of labor, which may exist between husband and wife, goes far beyond any specific tasks. It involves an entire life style and cuts across the issues discussed so far. It encompasses the hostess role, housekeeping, child rearing, and more.

The most dramatic division between server and served appeared among the traditional couples. For example, in over half the traditional cases, a kind of relationship occurred which never occurred in such an extreme form in any professional couple. There was a very asymmetrical helping relationship. The wife organized her whole life in such a way as to support and further her husband's career, but did not receive any comparable kind of support from him. The husband's work was seen as so important and demanding of time and energy, that the wife had to do everything possible to free him from other distracting responsibilities.

One traditional woman described this division of labor as follows. She saw a serious conflict between the ambition of a woman and her position in the marriage. She said that having a career, in contrast to merely working per se, means long-range planning and ambition. A career is chancy. There is the constant question of whether one will make it. One must pour energy into it, and this is detracted from the resources of the family. She said:

> *There is a real structural difference between the role of a woman in the family and that of a man—there isn't any getting around it. The woman's role is structurally subordinate to that of the man, no matter how much equality exists as individuals. Women are in the position of being wife and mother. This is a stance that is exactly the opposite of a person pursuing their own ambition. A wife and mother has to spend a good deal of time in the position of serving the family, . . . of being in the role of server. And the one who serves — they are open to being called on at any time.*

She believed that most marriages could tolerate only one career, and many marriages not even that. A career absorbed a person's energies and left less for the family.

In those traditional cases where the helping relationship was very asymmetrical, many aspects of the wife's life were involved. In one traditional couple, for example, the wife followed the husband as he moved from job to job. She did all the housekeeping tasks herself. She also managed the family's money and did the yard work. She was responsible for buying the car and having it serviced; she did all the driving because the husband did not know how. In this particular couple, the husband was not even very involved with the children. She did leisure-time activities with the children, while he frequently worked all weekend. If she had to go out in the evening before the children were in bed, she got a baby sitter to look after them — even though the husband was at home. She said her husband was used to quite a bit of service and used to having her adjust to his hours. She said she had done everything she could to make things easy for him so he would have all the time available for his work. She thought if she returned to work there might be some problems over schedules — some competition for her time.

It is not surprising that this extreme kind of division of labor was never found among the two-career families. It would be almost impossible for a woman to conscientiously meet the demands of a professional job and simultaneously always be available and willing as servant to her husband.

The interviews suggest that there are three main outlets for the energies which highly educated women have. They can express themselves — their ambition, involvement, energy — in their own careers, or through involvement in the husband's career, or through their children. Given the high value placed on work in our society, the latter two alternatives can be considered only compensatory or vicarious. The professional women poured much of their energies into their own careers, although most also reared children and helped their husbands. In contrast, most traditional women, not having work of their own, poured their energies into their husbands' careers or their children. They made promotion of the husband a full-time job or they exhibited a high degree of maternal possessiveness.

NOTES

1. All societies so far have used sex as one of the bases for a division of labor. However, there is great variability between societies as to which tasks get assigned to which sex. What constitutes a man's task in one society may be defined as a woman's task in another. This tremendous variability has led Linton to suggest that the actual assignment of tasks, rather than being determined by biology, is almost entirely determined by culture. In support of this point, he cites some examples which are counter to our own expectations. Ralph Linton, *The Study of Man* (New York: Appleton-Century-Crofts, 1936), pp. 116-17. Nevertheless, some general trends have been reported. Murdock's data from 224 tribes suggest one cross-cultural trend. It is mobility that differentiates between men's and women's tasks. Tasks that tended to be assigned to women were ones which could be carried on in the house or its immediate environment. The tasks that tended to be assigned to men were tasks like herding and hunting, which took the men far away from the dwelling place. George Peter Murdock, *Social Structure* (New York: Free Press Paperback, 1965), p. 213. (First published 1949: Macmillian Co.) Goode, as discussed in the present chapter, reports another cross-cultural trend. Whatever the strictly male tasks are, they are defined as being more honorific. William J. Goode, *The Family* (Englewood Cliffs, New Jersey: Prentice-Hall, 1964), pp. 69-70.

2. *Ibid.*, p. 70 (Emphasis in the original).

3. Analysts in the Parsonian tradition have been the biggest promoters of the idea that sex roles differentiate along instrumental-expressive lines. See for example, Morris Zelditch, Jr., "Role Differentiation in the Nuclear Family: A Comparative Study." *Family, Socialization and Interaction Process*, by Talcott Parsons and Robert F. Bales and Associates (New York: Free Press, 1955), pp. 307-52. For a good critique see Eugene Litwak, with assistance from Josefina Figueira, "Technological Innovation and Ideal Forms of Family Structure in an Industrial Democratic Society." Paper read at the Ninth International Seminar on Family Research, Tokyo, Japan, September 14-20, 1965.

4. Everett Cherrington Hughes, "Dilemmas and Contradictions of Status," *Men And Their Work* (Glencoe, Ill.: Free Press, 1958), p. 106. Originally published in *American Journal of Sociology* 50 (March, 1945), pp. 353-59.

5. Cynthia Fuchs Epstein, *Woman's Place: Options and Limits In Professional Careers* (Berkeley: University of California Press, 1970), pp. 88-89. As another example, see the lively account of how one woman scientist was perceived in James D. Watson, *The Double Helix* (New York: New American Library Signet Book, 1969). (First published in 1968: New York, Atheneum). For comments on women in the social sciences, see Mintz' humorous article on male-female role expectations. Geraldine R. Mintz (pseud.), "Some Observations On the Function of Women Sociologists at Sociology Conventions," *The American Sociologist*, 2 (August, 1967), pp. 158-59. Letters in reply — both pro and con — were published two issues later.

6. Cynthia Fuchs Epstein, "Women and Professional Careers: The Case of the Woman Lawyer" (unpublished Ph.D. dissertation, Columbia University, 1968), pp. 254-56.

7. See the descriptions in William H. Whyte, Jr., "The Wives of Management," *Man, Work and Society*, eds. Sigmund Nosow and William H. Form (New York: Basic Books, 1962), pp. 548-55 (Abridged from *Fortune*, 1951); Morris Janowitz, *The Professional Soldier* (New York: Free Press, 1960), pp. 196-211; and Margaret L. Helfrich, "The Generalized Role of the Executive's Wife," *Marriage and Family Living*, 23 (November 1961), pp. 384-87.

8. Epstein, *Woman's Place*, p. 114.

9. See, for example, Pat Mainardi, "The Politics of Housework," *Sisterhood Is Powerful: An Anthology of Writings from the Women's Liberation Movement*, ed. Robin Morgan (New York: Random House Vintage Books, 1970), pp. 447-54.

10. To be precise, in slightly over a third of the couples, the husband did at least three of these nine housekeeping tasks at least half of the time.

11. For an interesting analysis of role interchangeability as a feature of the family structure in an industrial democratic society, see Litwak, *op. cit.*

12. The finding that couples cited practical reasons for allocating tasks is in keeping with the results of Blood and Wolfe. They report that families in their study were pragmatic in settling who did what around the house. They state that although traditional families exist, the question is whether they are traditional because of ideological reasons or matters of convenience. In trying to account for variations between families in their study, they conclude that it is pragmatic factors that provide workable interpretations for the data. Robert O. Blood, Jr. and Donald M. Wolfe, *Husbands and Wives: The Dynamics of Married Living* (New York: Free Press, 1960), p. 56.

13. Information is not available for all couples on these issues, since they were just brought up spontaneously in the conversation.

14. These findings are in keeping with the results of previous research. Studies have shown that when the wife is employed, various housekeeping tasks are shifted to husbands and/or to paid help and services. See the discussion in Robert O. Blood, "The Husband-Wife Relationship," *The Em-*

ployed Mother in America, by F. Ivan Nye and Lois Wladis Hoffman (Chicago: Rand McNally, 1963), p. 286.

15. Parsons is noted for emphasizing that the isolation of the conjugal family is the most striking feature of our kinship system. Talcott Parsons, "The Social Structure of the Family," *The Family: Its Function and Destiny,* ed. Ruth Nanda Anshen (New York: Harper, 1949), pp. 179-80. Subsequently, various researchers have shown ways in which Americans do retain ties with relatives beyond the nuclear family; for example, mutual aid is given and visits are made. See, for example, Marvin B. Sussman, "The Help Pattern in the Middle Class Family," *American Sociological Review,* 18 (February, 1953), pp. 22-28; Eugene Litwak, "Occupational Mobility and Extended Family Cohesion," *American Sociological Review* 25 (February, 1960) pp. 9-21. The fact remains, however, that despite such aid and visits, the nuclear family is on its own for getting through the day-to-day routine.

16. Philip E. Slater, *The Pursuit of Loneliness: American Culture At The Breaking Point* (Boston: Beacon Press, 1970), p. 67.

17. *Ibid.,* p. 68.

18. Benjamin Spock, *Baby and Child Care* (Rev. ed.; New York: Pocket Books, 1968), p. 564.

19. They were asked whether as a matter of principle they thought it was better for the child to be looked after always by its own mother or better to have other people for part of the time.

6

Allocation of Time, Effort, and Money

> *It was a bit rushed and hectic. . . .*
> *But ordinarily we have made it*
> *work pretty well by a kind of shar-*
> *ing of jobs, domestic and profes-*
> *sional.*
> *Husband, professional couple*

> *I operate a rather hectic schedule.*
> *And in that sense I feel that things*
> *have to be organized for me.*
> *Husband, traditional couple*

The two-career family may have to display considerable ingenuity to mesh the occupational and familial demands placed on it. This chapter discusses how those interviewed allocated their resources — such as time, energy, and money — so as to fulfill their responsibilities in both these worlds.

THE SCHEDULE

Acceptance of career goals makes time a scarce resource — limited in supply and greatly in demand. A serious career requires an expenditure of a great deal of time. Professional and managerial occupations are characterized by long hours of work both during training and later on the job. The absolute amount of time involved is not the only factor; the scheduling of such time is also important, and this time schedule may be awkward from the point of view of family responsibilities. There will be occasions when a person, in order to conscientiously fulfill his work obligations, will have to put family responsibilities in second place.

Jobs differ as to who controls the time schedule. In a number of professions individuals may have considerable control over their own time schedules and thus have great flexibility. Even so, part of the schedule will be controlled by other people or by objects: appointments with clients must be kept; classes have to be taught at a given hour; the scientific observer must adapt to the timing of his experiment. The need for periods of relatively uninterrupted time in which to devote full attention to work is another factor. It is difficult to pursue serious intellectual work if one only has brief and scattered periods in which to do so.

A family makes many time demands too, for it is hard to develop a meaningful relationship with another person — in this case a spouse or child — unless one devotes sufficient time to it. But the schedule imposed by a family may be awkward from the point of view of work responsibilities. Moreover, the time schedule of the family is also partly determined by other people — either by other family members' personal preferences or by outsiders who designate when other family members will be at work or at school. Conflicting schedules may even make it difficult to assemble the family at a given hour, such as for dinner.

The one-career family represents a division of labor as regards the multitude of activites that compete for time and attention. The husband's schedule is primarily determined by his work, and family responsibilities are fit into that. The wife's schedule is primarily determined by her family responsibilities, and any work of her own is fit into the family's routine. In the two-career family, scheduling problems may become more acute.

Pressures of Time

Most of the professional women interviewed felt pressed for time. This is not surprising in view of the multitude of activities that were competing for their attention. They made comments such as "when the alarm goes off in the morning it's like the horses off at the races." "The last couple of years of my life have been fantastically hectic." "The routine is one that would discourage anyone." "It's a constantly changing scrabble." One woman, even without children, spoke as follows of her job in the humanities:

> It is a very time-consuming job and the domestic side of life is sandwiched in. . . . The pressure of time is enormous. It's one of the very real disadvantages. In a position with an institution in the academic world,

the day does not end at five o'clock. You're not in full control over the disposition of your time and some weeks it is worse than others. . . . I get frantic over lack of time.

Acceptance of career goals in and of itself makes time scarce. No matter how much work one gets accomplished, one still has never "done enough." The addition of other activities then compounds the problem.

Most of the men also felt pressed for time. For example, one man described his schedule saying, "At least over the past year, in terms of time, our lives have been pretty much like a countdown for a rocket." The men indicated that they felt this pressure either because of their own work responsibilities, because of the time they felt their family demanded, or because of the complications from the fact that the wife also had a career.

Allocation of Time
The women, in particular, responded to the pressure of time by carefully organizing their use of this scarce resource. They budgeted time almost like one might budget money and were very conscious of how they allocated time and effort.[1] In part, schedules were imposed on them by other people, such as employers and family members, but most professional women elaborated their organization beyond these outside impositions. One woman described her routine as follows:

On a weekday we get up at 7:30 and process the children. . . . This semester I've been teaching three mornings. . . . I have had a babysitter who comes every weekday afternoon from 12:00 to 4:00. . . . One of us is home until noon, and then we're both [at the university] in the afternoon. . . . I go home at 4:00 and between 4:00 and 6:00 it's largely a matter of spending some time with the children and making preparations for dinner. We have a kind of family time just ahead of dinner. We relax over a drink. The little girl joins us. . . . After dinner I finish up with the house routine. . . . I usually clear it anywhere between 9:00 and 10:00. . . . I often don't get out of the kitchen until about 10:00. But anyway, at whatever point I do, I go to my study and I do my desk work. . . . I'm at my desk for about three hours every night, roughly 9:00 to 12:00. . . . For weekends, during the day Saturday and Sunday I again am with the children, and engage pretty much in household things unless there's something exceptional coming along as there often is — a meeting at the university. And again I do my desk work in the evening.

The specifics she mentioned may be idiosyncratic, but the quote is representative of the general tendency of the professional women to follow a routine. Various activities — different types of work-related activities, housekeeping tasks, and family relations — tended to be allotted to a certain regular time in a weekly schedule.

Most of the men in these couples followed a routine too — sometimes more complex than that of their wives. However, the men seldom reported that they consciously thought of certain hours as reserved for their family. Even though they might spend time with the family, only a few spoke of an explicit family routine. The women were more conscious of having to arrange specific hours for their family, especially during the weekdays. It was the women who were more apt to make comments like "I try to keep the hours from 4:00 to 6:00 open for the family." "I'm available from 2:30 until my daughter goes to bed." "From 6:00 until the time the children go to sleep, which is 9:00 or later, I'm a full-time mother."

Not only did most of these women have some routine, but a few went so far as to suggest that if a woman was not capable of being organized, then it probably would not be possible for her to pursue a career. One wife said:

> My primary word is organization. . . . A woman who wants to be in a profession needs physical vitality and needs to be well organized. And if you're not, I would hesitate to recommend it.

Only a few said they did things unsystematically. These seemed to have a set of priorities regarding what it was important to do. But the schedule of when these activities got done was on more of an *ad hoc* basis. None of the professional women, however, had the luxury of drifting casually from activity to activity as the day progressed.

Flexibility and Control Over the Schedule

Flexibility of hours and control over one's own work schedule are usually seen as highly desirable. These attributes of a job are especially important to a two-career family in which the parents are trying to carry on professional work and rear children. Control over one's hours is often more important than the absolute number of hours required by the job. For example, one woman described her routine as follows:

> I always planned to be at home in the afternoon when [my daughter] got home from school. I felt that was imperative. And I also tried as far as I could to be fairly flexible. That is, by three o'clock when the school bus stopped, to have only a couple of hours more work, which I could do either in the afternoon or the evening so that if she wanted something I would be free.

Working the same amount of time, but on a rigid schedule, would have made it more difficult for this woman to combine family and career.

Most of the professional women did have considerable control over a large proportion of their work routine. Although certain parts of the day were dominated by regularly scheduled work, the rest of the schedule was up to them. They saw this as a great advantage. Only a few women with small children worked, or had worked, all year round on a full-time rigid work schedule such as 8:00 to 5:00; and even among these few women who did, two made arrangements to arrive at work an hour late or leave, if necessary, an hour early.

Control over one's domestic work schedule is also helpful. The two domestic tasks which were most awkward for the women, from the point of view of their professional work routine, were ones that they were expected to do at specific times. These tasks were cooking dinner and being home when the children got out of school. For example, one woman said:

[Cooking dinner] is one of the big difficulties because I have found that I tend to work well in the late afternoon and not well in the morning. So it's tough on me to leave the office at 6:00 and then come home and start cooking dinner.

Several women mentioned problems in connection with the dinner hour — apparently because they seldom delegated the cooking to anyone else and the family expected them to be home on time to cook it. Most of the women's colleagues — being men — did not work under this scheduling constraint.

Meshing Two Schedules

Not only do career goals make the husband and the wife each busy as individuals, but there is also the additional problem of meshing together the schedules of these two busy people. The sexual division of labor that is possible in the one-career family — where the husband's routine is planned around his work and the wife's around the household — is not possible for the two-career family. Thus the scheduling problems are more acute. And there is a dual aspect to them.

On the one hand, if one marital partner is preoccupied with a career, it would seem desirable for the other partner also to have a career so as to have something to occupy the time. Several people mentioned this aspect. One man, for example, commented as follows:

In the early part of our careers, we'd both study like fiends. We'd have dinner and work in separate rooms until 2:00 a.m. If either had not had a career it would have been difficult to mutually understand. I see this happen with my students — where there is a married student and his wife wants to get out and do things.

A few other husbands mentioned that they had more of a chance to do their professional work because their wives were busy with their own work.

On the other hand, having a second career in the family may add to scheduling difficulties. Here there are two levels of possible difficulty. Besides the practical problem of meshing the schedules of two very busy people, there is the attitudinal aspect. The expectation in the general society is that the husband's time has priority, and the wife is supposed to "be available" and fit her life into his time schedule. Both these aspects are illustrated in the following quote.

> *I usually write out a written schedule of what I'm going to do that day. In fact I have a calendar and it has what I'm going to do that day, and anything I know that's coming is on that calendar. [My husband] has a similar one, because where we have two careers, often times I'm required to attend some functions for him and I have to know about it, and he has to know about what I'm doing, to keep this thing balanced.*

This couple experienced the practical problems of matching two calendars, and also the wife was expected to be available to attend certain functions "as a wife."

The difficulty of matching two busy calendars, and the time pressure created by two careers, can be illustrated by other findings too. Several couples reported that the husband and wife had competed with each other for time or for whose schedule would get priority. For example, one woman reported that she and her husband had not competed professionally but had fought consistently about time commitments.

In addition, several couples reported some concern about the wife not being sufficiently available to spend time with her husband. Several wives made comments like "He says, 'I don't see you very often,'" or "There are times that I do feel torn, that I should be spending time with him," or "He does like me to be available in the evenings should he want not to work." Furthermore, in addition to daily or weekly scheduling difficulties, seven couples reported other scheduling problems such as difficulty in finding a weekend when both husband and wife were free to get away.

The presence of children increases the complexities of scheduling. There are no longer just the schedules of two persons but those of three or more people to coordinate. In general, the husband as well as the wife is affected by this. Most of the fathers interviewed — even those on rather rigid work schedules — had had to pinch hit at home for their wives at least occasionally; for example, they had done things like stay home half the day when the couple was unexpectedly "sitter-less." A few husbands who had flexible work schedules had been willing and able to do a lot of their work at home and to do a large share of the babysitting, taking turns with their wives. The following case illustrates both the complexities of scheduling, as well as the increased difficulties caused by an emergency. In this couple, normally the husband and wife took turns staying home in the morning; both could be away in the afternoon when the sitter was there. But recently, their plan had been upset by the sitter's illness.

> *What happened three weeks ago was that [the babysitter] suddenly needed to go to the hospital. . . . From that point on to the present we've been whirling around trying to make the thing go, with two kids. . . . We've managed to eke it out. . . . When the last day of classes occurred on Tuesday, we were both pretty well able to sigh and say, "Thank God, it's over." It was a bit rushed and hectic. . . . But ordinarily we have made it work pretty well by a kind of sharing of jobs, domestic and professional.*

This couple's already busy schedule became even more rushed and hectic because of the babysitter's illness. If a two-career family relies on hired help "to make the thing go," such lapses may place increased burdens on both the husband and the wife. This couple's experience shows, once again, how the problems associated with two careers in a family affect not only the women but also the men.

To more fully understand the routine of a two-career family, one would also have to consider the impact of the child's schedule once he or she is old enough to engage in activities outside the home. As one woman said:

> *You probably don't fully appreciate what having an eleven to twelve year old child is like — the social schedule and the schedule involved in two kinds of music lessons and an interest in the drama and possibly swimming lessons in the spring, and now we're involved in orthodontia. . . . We keep a very complicated calendar at home, which I'm happy to say, she's trained to use.*

Of course, given the lack of public transportation in many middle-class residential areas, these activities outside the home require an adult to provide transportation for the child. Also, once the child is in school, the parents may not only have to plan their traveling in terms of when they can get away together, but they may also have to consider the child's school calendar.

Modified Work Schedules
Modifying work schedules was another technique used, primarily by

women, to deal with the pressures of time and scheduling in the two-career family. As mentioned previously, half the professional women had at some point altered study or employment schedules in order to fulfill family responsibilities. They reduced the amount of time they worked, or they departed from the normal routine as regards which particular hours they would work. For example, one woman arrived three quarters of an hour late to work each day, but then made up this lost time by working on some of the days when she normally would have gotten vacation. She said:

> I have another thing that I do so that in my own mind and their minds I'm not taking advantage of them. I have never taken my full vacation time. I sort of figure out roughly what, over the year, I'm abusing, and I make that up by working those days off, so nobody will think I'm putting anything over on anybody.

This case is interesting because it shows how just a very small modification — just a three-quarter hour deviation from the normal schedule — really made it possible for this woman to fulfill work and family responsibilities. And it shows, once again, how flexibility of the schedule is often more important to a professional woman than the absolute number of hours she is required to work.

Some women commented on whether or not a woman should be given special consideration. Their tendency was to stress not letting the family interfere. For example, one said:

> I'm very — perhaps overly — sensitive and cautious about not letting the fact that I am a woman and have certain responsibilities interfere. . . . I find that I miss much less than some young men with young children and families. . . . I bend over backwards not to miss anything. I have never given a domestic excuse for anything, and certainly not to expect any consideration because I am a female. And I think that has been recognized and respected.

The tendency was to be hyper-conscientious, rather than to criticize the system as being too demanding. Even when special favors were granted — like the privilege of arriving at work a little late — the tendency was to compensate for this by very conscientiously fulfilling responsibilities. This pattern of women in professional settings being hyper-conscientious also appeared in a recent study of lawyers. "Women lawyers . . . feel the need to demonstrate their worth to colleagues, and perhaps to themselves, by over-working." In trying to make up for women's second-class status in the legal profession, women attorneys tend to over-react. "They often over-produce and exhibit other types of 'compulsive' behavior and 'over-conformity' reactions typical of" people striving for achievement, even though placed in a situation where many opportunities are closed to them.[2]

The Traditional Couples

The traditional women did not conform to any one pattern regarding how they actually used their time. They either pleasantly drifted from activity to activity, organized their schedule so as to return to work or school part time, or were so harassed by domestic responsibilities that they never had an hour completely free.

Traditional women did see clearly the difference between working and not working as to the amount of organization that is required. They saw that employment requires a person to follow more of a routine. One wife, for example, said her return to part-time work had forced her onto a schedule. In general, she enjoyed the return to work. But at times, the schedule seemed too rigorous:

> *Sometimes managing this is at the expense of an awful lot of physical energy. I sometimes am very tired. I work harder at being with the children and making use of my time with them, and planning it, and the same with the groceries you know. . . . I'm a lot more pushed to keep onto some kind of schedule. I sometimes find that I'd just like to relax and forget the whole business (laughter).*

As another example, a woman who was thinking of returning to work, saw that in the future she would just have to plan her day from morning to night. She said there's a very pleasant feeling about just drifting sometimes. She saw she wouldn't have much opportunity to do that in the future if she worked.

A major difference between the professional group and the traditional group was how they matched calendars of the husband and of the wife. In the professional group, the wife's own schedule was an important factor to be taken into account, whereas in the traditional group it was not. Among the professional group there were many couples where it was not completely clear cut whose schedule took precedence. And even in the professional couples where there were indications the husband's schedule should or did take precedence, the wife's plans nevertheless did alter the meshing of the two schedules. In contrast, among almost all the traditional couples, the husband's work schedule clearly took precedence over the wife's schedule and also dominated the family routine. In one of the more extreme traditional cases, the wife described the situation as follows:

> *He has the kind of schedule that gets first consideration in this house. He happens to be very busy. He does a lot of traveling and there are many*

*demands on his time. And whatever I do, it has to fit in with what he
requires of me. Mine will never be the first career in this house. I will not
be his (laughter) competitor in terms of time and effort. . . . I do have to
be sufficiently flexible to fit in with his schedule.*

The husband, when asked if he would mind if his wife traveled for
professional business, first replied that it would be all right; but then,
as he realized it might influence his schedule, he commented as follows:

*I operate a rather hectic schedule. And in that sense I feel that things
have to be organized for me. I suppose in that sense I might [object] if
something were to occur that could possibly upset the sort of hair-line
schedule that I run. So I'd find [my wife's traveling] objectionable.*

The husband's work schedule also dominated family routine. For example, he was frequently late for dinner, and the family waited for
him. The wife said sometimes this did bother her, "But, it's something
that even the children have learned at this stage to expect and accept."
This particular traditional husband was very conscientious about
spending time with his family; however, the choice of when to do this
was very much up to him. The emphasis was on the worth of the husband's time and the cheapness of the housewife's time.

PRIORITIES OF THE PROFESSIONAL WOMEN

The professional women were very conscious about having to make
choices. They recognized that there is not enough time or energy to
do all that one might want to do. A person must set priorities. Some
of their priorities have already been discussed; for example, certain
professional activities they gave up in order to have families. Here,
the opposite question is discussed: What, if anything, has a woman
had to give up in order to have a career?

Most of these women had given up activities or made other sacrifices in order to pursue their careers. One described this as follows:

*The day has just so many hours and . . . there is just so much energy to
do things. Something has to give somewhere. And in my case it has had
to be social life where I've had to cut pretty much to a minimum. I have
very many good friends that I just don't get to see. . . . I just don't have
the time to fit everything in. . . . I would like to do some things in creative
arts. For years I've had a desire to do work in ceramics and to take weav-
ing. . . . I studied [music] for about 10 or 15 years. But all that I just don't
have time for. . . . And I have an interest in politics, but I feel I just can't
get involved in outside work . . . so I have to be in a certain sense almost*

a passive citizen. Again, because of the limitations of time and to what will I give priority at the moment.

The particular things this woman mentioned giving up are idiosyncratic; there were women who kept up in these activities, but gave up other things like community involvement, gardening, a smoothly run house, leisure reading. Many of the women also made sacrifices in terms of physical fatigue, too. Over half the professional women mentioned having problems, at least some time in their careers, of not having enough energy, of fatigue, of being tired and weary in a physical sense.[3]

Having the career in the first place already implies setting priorities, since these women worked "by choice" rather than "out of necessity." They pursued their professions because it brought them some kind of gratification, whether personal satisfaction or the satisfaction of social contributions. There were of course, moments of great discouragement, and a few mentioned that when tired or pressured, they occasionally wondered "why bother?" As one commented, "What does it really amount to — another article published that nobody's going to read ten years from now." But such statements appeared to reflect passing thought in a moment of discouragement or fatigue, rather than any really serious desire to quit their profession.

THE USE OF MONEY

One usually works, among other reasons, in order to make money. However, the complexities of two careers in one family are such that the second career, in terms of net income, is not necessarily a source of much additional money. In some cases or at some point in her career, the wife may actually be paying for the privilege of being able to work; here, family resources may have to be arranged so as to finance her career.

The Willingness to Use Money

Professional couples were willing to use money to help solve the difficulties posed by two careers. And the single biggest expense associated with two careers is payment for hired help, especially for child care. Asked how they felt about this expense, most said either that they could afford to pay or that it was just something a woman had to do if she wanted to work. For example, one woman explained as follows about how having a lot of money made it easier to have a career:

Having a good deal of money makes this easier. I am a realist when it comes to matters of money. . . . I feel no sense of uneasiness over a nurse. . . . And I can pay. I have the money. I ask, what are the wages that I'll have to pay that will get me what I want. It doesn't depend on my budget.

She said she knew what she wanted as regards competent help, and she had the money to pay to get it. In another couple, the husband replied as follows:

Most women I know who do work probably use up most of their salary on these expenses. They're working because they're serious about their work. They're not making money on it. Or they're making a little bit, but usually damn little. And I think the issue there is perfectly clear. If a woman is, you know, is serious in her interest, that's what she'll do.

Professional couples also used money in a great variety of other ways to save time and effort and to make two careers possible. For example, in one couple, the complications of scheduling time were eased by the purchase of a second car. The wife explained, "Having only one car is a real psychological hardship because we work at different rhythms and we don't like to wait for each other." Another couple was willing to pay a higher price for the privilege of living close to work. The husband explained, "We've always preferred to pay for [living close] because we think it's a tremendous saving in time and energy." Moreover, in several couples the women used money to ease the burdens imposed by the hostess role. One woman explained:

[My husband] feels strongly . . . that I should be willing to pay to get things done. . . . There was a time when I was chairman and found getting dinner for guests and that kind of thing difficult. We sometimes entertain in restaurants. We took people out and we felt it was worth the expense, so that I would not have to do all the work. . . . He thinks that since we do have the money, we should spend it.

The details varied from couple to couple regarding what particular problems of two careers were eased with money. But the general trend was to be in favor of spending money if it would ease the situation.

The professional couples' ability to use money to offset the difficulties of two careers was related to their relatively high income level. Most of them, when interviewed, had total family incomes, before taxes, of over $20,000 a year. And slightly over a third of these couples had a family income of $30,000 or higher. Slightly over half of the professional wives themselves made between $10,000 and $20,000 a year. And the wife with the highest earned income made between $25,000 and $30,000 annually.[4] It is not surprising that, when interviewed, many replied that they could afford help and the other costs of working. The few real hardships they reported regarding such expenses referred to their early years; for example, those who had children early and needed to pay for child care before their earning capacity was very high. It must be remembered that most of these women had their first child relatively late in life, and, had they started their families at an earlier age or earlier stage in their careers, the financial hardships would have been more acute. In a recent study of female physicians there were some women who married prior to finishing their medical training. And since they tended to marry physicians who were also in training, neither spouse had a solid income at the time. Among these, the ones with children complained about the difficulty of making arrangements for child care and about the cost of such care.[5]

The Traditional Couples

The traditional women indicated that financial considerations were not the main reason for deciding to work or not work. They said that a second career did not necessarily add a great deal to the family income because of the costs involved in working. They made comments such as, "Financially, you're lucky if you just break even." "As long as I break even, and make perhaps a little extra, I would be happy." Perhaps the situation was best summed up by a woman who had recently returned to part-time work. She said, "I think it's marvelous to work, but you have to be very affluent to be able to."

The Double Standard in Accounting

There are two levels on which one can examine the use of money in connection with two careers. One is the reality level. Some costs are, in reality, tied directly to having two careers. Child care is the best example. It is a fact that in the middle-class family, the costs of hired help for child care are enormously increased if both spouses work.

A second level is how the people perceive the use of money and how they account for it mentally. The tendency is to do a very asymmetrical job of accounting. There is a double standard. The logic applied to the income of the wife is different than the logic applied to the income of the husband. The difference in logic is congruent with the difference in expectations as to whether men should work vs. whether women should work.

It is expected that a husband will work. Expenses associated with his work are perceived as automatically legitimate; sometimes the link is not even made between the costs and his working. It is more of a choice for a woman to work. And mentally, many costs are perceived as tied to her working. For example, one professional woman described as follows how the costs associated with her working were so great that, despite her relatively high income bracket, her net income was very low:

> [My husband] sat down and figured out one day . . . that when you consider household help, second car, professional clothes, my higher income tax bracket, the whole bit — and I was earning in the $10,000 a year category at that time — that I was making about 10c an hour. So that you can't say that it's a matter of bringing home a good second salary.

This is "faulty accounting" for at least two reasons. First of all, the items in the quote — help, car, clothes — have an independent desirability. They may be necessary for her to work; but they are also pleasant in themselves. Yet despite their independent desirability, these items get subtracted from her income. They become part of an argument alleging that it really is not financially profitable for her to work. In contrast, things like a car which the husband's job requires — but which also have independent desirability — do not get viewed in the same way. They are not incorporated into an argument alleging that it is not financially profitable for him to work. An extreme example of this would be the man with the type of career that requires a show-place home for entertaining clients and associates. One does not commonly hear it said that the show-place is so expensive that it really does not pay for him to work. Secondly, the accounting in the above quote is "faulty" in that many of the items she links to her working are items which housewives also spend money on. For example, typically the suburban housewife needs a car, because of the physical layout of the community, to be a housewife. Thus, the issue of whether it is financially profitable for a wife to work is not only a matter of reality factors. It is also a matter of perception.

NOTES

1. Everett Hughes calls this a person's "economy of time and effort." He has developed this concept, and the related one of "level and direction of effort" in his research; for example, in his analyses of student culture. See Howard S. Becker *et. al.*, *Boys in White: Student Culture in Medical School* (Chicago: Univ. of Chicago Press, 1961); and, Howard S. Becker, Blanche Geer, and Everett C. Hughes, *Making the Grade: The Academic Side of College Life* (New York: Wiley, 1968).

2. Cynthia Fuchs Epstein, "Women and Professional Careers: The Case of the Woman Lawyer" (unpublished Ph.D. dissertation, Columbia University, 1968), pp. 246-47.

3. In thinking of the advantages and disadvantages of careers, one should remember that busy people are not the only ones who may suffer from fatigue. People who are bored with their lives because of having little that is meaningful to do also often report fatigue. One thinks, for example, of the so-called "tired housewife syndrome" reported in the literature.

4. These people, to use Miller's terms, certainly were not the "rich-rich". But, they nevertheless were in the higher income brackets when interviewed in 1968. A comparison with Miller's analysis of income distribution in the U. S., even though his figures are from 1960, still gives one a general idea of how they fit into the overall picture. Miller discusses the characteristics of the wealthiest 5 per cent of the families and also of the top 1 per cent. In 1960 a family with an income of more than $15,000 a year was in the top 5 per cent and a family with $25,000 a year was in the top 1 per cent. Miller is, incidentally, talking of family income. The figures for various members of the family were pooled together. Herman P. Miller, *Rich Man Poor Man* (New York: New American Library Signet Book, 1965), p. 137. (First published in 1964: New York, Thomas Y. Crowell Co.)

5. Jane Gaudette Jones, private communication.

7

Competitiveness

We identify very much with each other. . . . We will be in competition together against some other person, not in competition with each other.

Professional wife

I do occasionally feel just a little resentment as to my role as opposed to my husband's role.

Traditional wife

Professional competition between husband and wife is a controversial topic on which emotions run high. Does full participation of both husband and wife in the occupational world necessarily lead to competitive feelings between them? The conventional answer is that it does. The mass media are full of dire warnings about the battle of the sexes that will ensue if women have careers. Many academic theorists support the position that if both a husband and wife pursue careers, this will lead to competition between them and disrupt the marriage. This argument, although not founded on solid evidence, has given an illusion of scientific support to the more popular views, and it has had an enormous impact on popular thinking. For this reason it is examined in detail below. Later it will be seen that information from the present study challenges, rather than supports this theory.

THE EXISTING THEORY

The one-career family is seen, by several influential theorists, to be *"the solution"* for eliminating disruptive competition between husband

and wife. One of the most important sociologists to push this view is Talcott Parsons, who believes that it is necessary to exclude wives from occupations commensurate with those of their husbands in order to preserve the solidarity of the family. To use his words, he believes that the solidarity of the conjugal family "is facilitated by the prevalence of the pattern that normally only *one* of its members has an occupational role which is of determinate significance for the status of the family as a whole."[1] It is thus important that the woman is exclusively a housewife or that she at most has a "job" rather than a "career." The crux of his argument is as follows:

> By confining the number of status-giving occupational roles of the members of the effective conjugal unit to one, it eliminates any competition for status, especially as between husband and wife, which might be disruptive of the solidarity of marriage. So long as lines of achievement are segregated and not directly comparable, there is less opportunity for jealousy, a sense of inferiority, etc. to develop.[2]

There are a number of shortcomings in Parsons' theory. One of the most notable is that he does not distinguish between being placed in a situation of competition, and feeling competitive about it. He sees these two things as so correlated that he never talks of their independent occurrence. He assumes that if people are placed "in competition," they will feel competitive about it, and he assumes that if they are not allowed to be in a situation of competition, they will not feel competitive toward each other. In contrast, the present analysis contends that being "in competition" and "feeling competitive" are independent and do not have any necessary relationship to each other.

The distinction between "in competition" and "feelings of competitiveness" was made long ago by those two early pioneers of American sociology, Robert E. Park and Ernest W. Burgess. Competition, they state, is not necessarily a hostile contention, and it is not necessarily something of which the competing individual is always conscious. They give an example of two people, A and B, who are under consideration for an appointment; A is chosen. "Neither of the two need know anything about the matter until the selection is made. It is eligibilty to perform some social function that makes a man a competitor, and he may or may not be aware of it, or, if aware of it, he may or may not be consciously opposed to others."[3] To Park and Burgess' discussion one should merely add that the opposite can also occur: a hostile contention may exist even though in actual fact the person may be excluded from the competition. For example, there might also be a third person, C, who, although not eligible and not being considered for the appointment, nevertheless knows about it, would like to have it, and feels competitive toward those who are actually being considered.

This distinction between being "in competition" and "feeling competitive" seems to be a useful one. However, it is completely lacking in Parsons' theory of occupational and family roles. He simply assumes that if put in a situation of competition, the spouses will feel competitive, and if not in such a situation, they will not have such feelings. In other words, he is making two assumptions. First of all, he assumes that if both husband and wife have careers, they will feel competitive with each other; that is, if placed "in competition" they will feel a sense of competition. He never considers other mechanisms which might prevent such feelings, even though the sex roles are not segregated — even though the marital partners are involved in activities similar to each other. He never considers that couples might segregate their marital life from their two careers by separation in time, separation in place, or by psychological compartmentalization, and he never considers the possibility that perhaps they simply do not define each other as competitors. Secondly, Parsons assumes that segregated sex roles do prevent competitiveness; that is, if the marital partners do different activities and thus are not placed "in competition," they will not feel a sense of competition, make invidious comparisons, or feel inferior. He assumes that if one spouse is "not allowed to play the game," such feelings with be automatically prevented. He never considers the possibility that since occupational achievement is more valued in our society than fulfillment of familial responsibilities, perhaps the wife will be upset over not even getting to enter the occupational world — over not even getting to play the game, over being relegated to the less prestigious line of achievement.

According to Parsons' theory of the necessity for a sex-linked division of labor, feelings of competitiveness should have occurred in the professional group and not occurred in the traditional group. However, the experiences of the couples interviewed were not in accordance with the predictions of this theory.

DID THE COUPLES FEEL COMPETITIVE?

In most of the two-career couples, the husband and wife said that they did not feel competitive toward each other. Specifically, thirteen of the twenty professional couples reported an absence of such feelings, and throughout their interviews there were no indications to the contrary. In a minority of professional couples, namely five, a sense of competition was reported by at least one spouse. And two couples' responses were ambiguous: while they reported that they did not experience a sense of competition, their descriptions of their lives gave indications to the contrary.

Of course, when dealing with social-psychological issues — in this case competitiveness — there is always the possibility of repression or suppression. The impulses may be excluded from one's consciousness and operate only on the unconscious level. A problem may exist even though it is not mentioned to the interviewer. Nevertheless, as with any sensitive social-psychological topic, one way the researcher tries to get at it is by looking at what people say when interviewed. This involves not only looking at answers they give to direct questions about competitive feelings, but also reviewing the entire interview and carefully "reading between the lines." This is what was done when analyzing this issue.

COMPETITIVENESS IN SAME VS. DIFFERENT FIELDS

Competitiveness did not correlate with whether the spouses were in the same or different fields. If one follows the Parsonian line of reasoning, one might predict that such feelings would be more likely if the husband and wife were in the same field. Here "same field" might either be defined as being within a given named discipline or defined in terms of the actual content of the work. Under such circumstances, the husband and wife would each be qualified to make direct professional judgments of each other's work. Under such conditions the sex roles would not be segregated at all. However, among professional couples, the presence or absence of competitive feelings did not seem to have anything to do with whether the spouses were in the same or in different lines of professional endeavor.

COMPETITIVENESS AND RELATIVE RATES OF SUCCESS

This society now equates masculinity with superiority, and femininity with inferiority. If the sexes do different activities, it is the men who are expected to do the more prestigeful ones. If they do the same activity, men are supposed to be better at it. And this expectation holds not just for work but for any activity that a man wishes to be good at.

The cultural norm that the man is supposed to win has been discussed by many authors — by social critics, researchers, and magazine writers. Marya Mannes has written on the social expectation that it is always the man who is supposed to be superior in an intellectual conversation with a woman. Many men do not want a woman to question their views. A woman with ideas is somewhat of a social embarrassment. Marya Mannes explains:

> People like us, therefore, must learn to keep a respectful silence in the presence of men who may have a higher or lower intelligence, or speak our minds at the risk of the glassy male eye. So here we are again, supposedly intelligent and gifted women, scared of losing our femininity by the simple measure of saying what we think — and know.[4]

Recent research shows how deeply internalized these cultural expectations are. Matina Horner's psychological research on the achievement motive shows that the intelligent woman is in a double bind: she not only worries about failure but also about success. Horner talks both of the achievement motive and the motive to avoid success. The latter she defines as "the fear that success in competitive achievement situations will lead to negative consequences, such as unpopularity and loss of femininity."[5] Horner presented college students with a statement about a person of their own sex who has just achieved the top score in the class. She asked them to write a brief story about what then happened to this person. She analyzed their answers to see if they contained imagery indicating strong fears of social rejection because of success, guilt over success and related doubts about one's normality, or complete denial that a person of one's own sex could be successful. Over 65 per cent of the girls, but less than 10 per cent of the boys showed evidence of the motive to avoid success.

Competitiveness and the need to make sure that the male wins are issues that the women's magazines trade upon. To cite just one example, a recent issue of the *Ladies' Home Journal* explains that skiing is a very feminine sport — but not if one does it aggressively and competitively. The expert male skier, Jean-Claude Killy, warns that "when a woman is too aggressive in sports, she passes beyond femininity. I admire courage, but the competition skier is not my kind of woman."[6] His comment parallels Mary Mannes' analysis. Women lose their femininity if they talk as intelligently or ski as expertly as men.

The converse is that many men feel that they lose their masculinity when a woman no longer acts inferior — when she does an activity as well as a man does it, especially one that is defined as so prestigious or difficult that only a man can do it. The male reaction may be that "she's not really a woman." Or men may say that she degraded the activity by doing it. A recent example is the furor over the first female football pro. In August, 1970, Mrs. Pat Palinkas served as place-kick holder in a minor-league game. She fumbled the first snap, but successfully caught and placed later ones. The comments of the opposing team's players are of more interest than her performance *per se*. They said quite explicitly that they felt she was "prancing around making folly with a man's game," and that having her play "degraded football."[7]

The general cultural norm of male superiority is also seen in marriage. The husband is expected to do the more prestigious activity, or, if he does the same activity as his wife, he is expected to do it better. The norm in marriage is that the husband should be superior to his wife in any activity he wishes to be good at — whether it be in the occupational world, social activities, athletics, or even a traditional feminine domain such as the culinary arts. From this point of view, "avoidance of competition" does not mean that the sexes do not compete; rather, it means that the husband should be more successful than the wife. Thus, one might predict a greater likelihood of competitive feelings if the wife was more professionally successful than the husband by any one of a number of criteria; for example, finishing her graduate education first, earning more money, having a higher ranking job, working at a more distinguished institution or company. Such circumstances violate the cultural norm that the husband should be more successful than the wife.

Among the professional group on any given measure of success, there were only one or two cases where the wife was ahead of her husband at some point in time or where the wife was ultimately more occupationally successful. Thus, there were not enough cases to determine if there is a positive correlation between the presence of feelings of competition and the wife being more successful. A larger sample would probably include more such cases, and it is predicted that such a positive correlation would occur.

Some support for this notion is provided by Cynthia Epstein's study of female lawyers. Epstein states that "it is expected that women be of *equal* social rank and of *lower* or equal occupational rank [than their husbands]."[8] If a woman does not remain in a subordinate position, she violates the expectations associated with being a wife and a female. Problems may result — for the couple and for their relationship with others — if the wife achieves more:

> There seems to be no precedent for cases where the wife rises in the occupational sphere and the husband does not since the cases are few. This is not to say that such cases do not exist. It is interesting to note that when they occur — as in the Negro middle-class where many women outrank

their husbands professionally — the situation is regarded as a case of social pathology.[9]

In Epstein's study, five wives outranked their husbands. They were uneasy about possessing the higher occupational rank. One actually defined it as a problem, saying it led to stress and divorce. The others felt it necessary to explain away the reasons for the inequality and to excessively extoll the achievements of their husbands. Thus, Epstein's study suggests that, at present, uncomfortable and uneasy feelings are associated with the wife achieving greater occupational success.

In summary, the present study suggests that the central issue in explaining the presence or absence of competitiveness is not whether the spouses do different or do the same activities. In other words, it is not a question of segregated vs. non-segregated sex roles. Rather, the central issue is that the cultural norm dictates that the husband has to be superior. The sexes are already engaged in a race, and the man is to win. Moreover, the cultural norm dictates that the husband should be superior to his wife — not only in work activities but in any way important to him.[10]

COMPETITIVENESS AND OTHER SUBJECTIVE FEELINGS

Whereas competitiveness toward the spouse did not correlate with what fields the husband and wife were in, it did correlate with other social-psychological traits. Feelings of competition, especially among the men, were associated with other feelings such as lack of self-assurance, feeling threatened, not feeling competent in a given area, feeling inadequate, or "pride of the male ego." In one case competitiveness with the wife seemed to be part of the husband's general tendency to engage in "one-ups-manship" intellectual games. It must be remembered that it is quite possible for a person to feel unsure or feel threatened, even though an outside observer would say that in objective terms the person's career is progressing very well or that the person has achieved success.

A social-psychological view of competitiveness suggests that it would be quite possible for only one of the marital partners to experience these feelings. Within the five professional couples where competitiveness clearly occurred at some time, these feelings vis-à-vis the spouse occurred more among the men than among the women. In some cases the wife was aware of how her husband felt; in other cases she was oblivious. The pair of quotes below illustrates the latter situation. The husband and wife were in different fields. Asked if the wife's career had led to a sense of competition between them, they replied as follows:

No. I never felt it, because he was always ahead (laughter) of the game, always ahead of me. . . . I don't think he has either. . . . I don't think it would [lead to competition] even if we were [in the same field] because I'm very relaxed about the whole thing. It just wouldn't bother me. . . . I don't feel competitive toward my colleagues either. I always feel I'm in a different kind of category. There aren't any women actually in the field. And then because I go part time. . . . I just don't really think in those terms.

(wife's interview)

I guess it may have. Not very often. As long as I'm able to do my work and do it well I don't really feel too much threatened by her. If we were in the same field I guess it would be pretty bad. . . . One time I had a manuscript rejected and something else was going along slowly and I think I must have felt, you know, a little inadequate. . . . But for the most part it's not been bad. . . . Her book was reviewed in [the newspaper]. . . . I would have felt jealous frankly except for the fact that my book had been reviewed. . . . But as long as I feel that I'm capable of standing on my own feet, then whatever she can do, so much the better. . . . I mean I'm pleased enough with my own work that I don't feel threatened by it. If somebody would say, "Well, she's pulling him along," that would be tough. But she's not, because I think I'm keeping my own.

(husband's interview)

Although the wife really did not think in competitive terms, it is obvious that the husband did, and, as the quote indicates, he felt this particularly when some of his own work was going slowly. In this couple the husband was always clearly ahead of his wife — always had the higher ranking job, earned more money, and published more. But it was of tremendous importance to him to prove that he could stand on his own two feet.

FOCUS OF THE COMPETITIVENESS

If competitiveness vis-à-vis the spouse is experienced by either the husband or the wife, almost anything can serve as a focal point of comparison. Couples who reported competitiveness, or gave indications of it, mentioned a great range of things that they compared; for example, who received more attention at a work-affiliated social gathering, who received greater newspaper publicity, who had a more flexible work schedule and more control over the hours of work, who had had their book reviewed in a more prestigious journal or newspaper, who wrote more pages or had more publications, who received more grants, who became successful faster or achieved a higher level of success as measured by a variety of criteria. When competitiveness occurs the "choice" of a particular attribute as a focal point of comparison is random or arbitrary — anything will do. Moreover, as the above list shows, one can make comparisons even using indirect indicators of the person's professional reputation and intellectual prowess.

The reputation of one's spouse among his or her colleagues is another source of indirect information which is of potential use for comparisons. In a few cases, for example, the husband explained how he knew his wife was highly regarded among her colleagues. The husband, being in a different field, could not judge the wife's work directly. But he accepted the indirect information from her colleagues. If a person feels competitive, this kind of indirect information can also be used to make comparative judgments. The following quote really illustrates the crux of the issue. This husband made comparisons with his wife, despite the fact that their fields were very different, and even though professionally they had segregated roles:

We've both become fairly successful and we've done this at approximately the same time. . . . Her promotions at [the university] were somewhat delayed because she is a woman. There's little doubt that she's as competent or more competent as other people there. I've heard this from enough sources. . . . Perhaps she's done more original work in her field than I've done in my field. I assume this from what I've heard. I've never been able to judge her work.

This particular husband's response was somewhat mixed. He said he had not experienced a sense of competition because of his wife's career. but he also said it was very important that he too had been able to achieve professional success at about the same rate his wife did. When first asked about feelings of competition, he said, "I'm sure that is one of your most important questions." He thought a man with a professional wife had to be self-assured so as to not feel challenged, and he said he felt self-assured. But he also saw where the challenge might present problems: "A number of my contemporaries are now divorced — couples where both had careers. I think they were unprepared to accept the relationship."

The fact that anything can serve as a focal point of comparison suggests why the presence or absence of competitiveness does not correlate with whether husband and wife are in the same or different fields. If a husband or wife wants to make comparative judgments vis-à-vis the spouse, it is not necessary to be able to evaluate the spouse's work directly. If one feels competitive, one can always find something to use as the basis of comparison. If the spouse is in a different field, one simply shifts the comparison to an indirect criterion, such as who has the greater reputation among colleagues. Or the competitiveness can even be carried out in some area other than work. One professional couple, for example, reported being competitive with each other when they engaged in voluntary political activities and even when they attended social gatherings. The interviews suggest that if a person feels competitive, something can always be found to use as the basis of comparison; and if a person does not feel competitive, many potential bases of comparison are overlooked.

EXPLANATIONS FOR NOT FEELING COMPETITIVE

Objectively competitiveness was found not to correlate with the similarity or dissimilarity of the husband's and wife's activities. But when the individuals were asked what prevented such feelings, a dissimilarity of activities was what they most often gave as the reason. In other words, when competitiveness did not occur, the people interviewed had their own perceived explanations of what prevented it. Most commonly, among both the women and the men, their explanation was that the marital partners did different things: they were in different fields; they were in different sub-fields; they did different parts of the problem when they worked together; their areas of competence were different; or they had different skills. As previously discussed, this line of reasoning did not hold up objectively. Thus within these couples where a sense of competition did not occur, it is as if at some subconscious level these people defined their situation in non-competitive terms.

This definition of their relationship in noncompetitive terms was expressed in several ways. For example, one couple thought of themselves as being members of the same team. They competed not against each other, but against outsiders. The wife explained why she thought they had not experienced competitiveness between themselves:

> I think because we identify very much with each other, and we look upon our work as joint work. That is, we will be in competition together against some other person, not in competition with each other.

Some couples defined their situation as being complementary rather than competitive. One man said:

> We have similar interests but we approach them from different points of view; we can strengthen each other rather than having to compete with each other.

Along a similar line another man said that he and his wife did not compete with each other "because they collaborated." He said, "It is rather an integration than competition." One couple's definition is particularly interesting because the wife was more successful occupationally than the husband. Asked about feelings of competition, he spoke as follows:

> There's never been any competition. . . . I mean we don't look at it this way. . . . I suppose I could feel embarrassed if I wanted to, but it isn't going to change anything to feel embarrassed. Sure I'd like to be able to equal it but I can't, and I never will, and I know I can't. I'm not going to waste my time wishing I could. . . . I don't think we're of that nature. . . . We are never competing for anything I can think of over the other, if you follow what I mean.

There were no indications elsewhere in the interview that competitiveness had been a problem. As to "sore points," he said that they had disagreed seriously only over the organization of time, but competitiveness did not seem to be a sore point. He spoke with considerable pride of his wife's accomplishments.[11]

There were other couples who defined their situation as being separate; not only were their fields originally separate, but they wanted to maintain the separation of interest. For example, in one couple, the husband and wife discussed general professional problems, but not the content of their respective disciplines. The husband explained:

> We don't know what the hell each other's doing really. Her work is quite different so I don't think we ever had any sense of competition. And you know, I'm always pleased and delighted when people take me aside and tell me how good she is. . . . But I mean fundamentally people don't get married to sit around and discuss their professional problems. . . . We discuss things, you know, and I know what she's doing. . . . But I think we like to keep this pretty separate.

Here the emphasis should be placed on their almost conscious attempt to maintain the separation of their two careers. They deliberately segmented the intellectual content of the careers from the rest of their relationship and the other things that they did discuss. They talked about general professional issues and served as "sounding boards" for each other, but they avoided detailed criticism and editing of each other's work.

The next most commonly offered explanation for lack of competitiveness concerned the relative rates of success of the spouses, or the husband's success. Several women said there was no sense of competition because the husband was ahead. One woman explained:

> There's no competition at all. He's considered one of the best people [in

his field] and it's just, you know, a very secure position, nothing I could compete with. . . . My husband is one of the best known people in the States, and you know, I'm just a regular, ordinary sort of college teacher.

Several men said there was no sense of competition because they were successful in their own careers. One explained:

I've never felt competitive with her. . . . I am always pleased by any particular kind of achievement on her part. . . . Since I don't feel frustrated, I don't feel any envy toward her. I feel I'm moving too. . . . You discover that when you talk about friction or envy or sense of competition, that too often results from a sense of personal failure on one person's part or the other. . . . But we haven't felt that way.

Other men talked of how they were self-assured in their own success or said that they were not being outstripped by the wife.

A few of the women mentioned the issue of competitiveness as being relevant to their choice of a marriage partner. One woman said she married her husband because he was smarter than she was and she knew she could never beat him. Another woman said she married her husband because he did not act competitively toward her in the way that other men had.

COPING WITH COMPETITIVE FEELINGS

A minority of professional couples did experience competitive feelings with respect to the spouse. Their competitiveness was most acute under certain specific conditions: when they discussed their work with each other, when they tried doing joint work, and when they attended social gatherings connected with the wife's work. The following quotes, taken from the couple who experienced the most severe feelings of competition, provide examples:

I think there's always been competition. . . . One relates a little differently to one's other colleagues than one does to one's spouse. We once tried writing something together and that was disastrous. . . . We just took the necessary argumentation personally. . . . [We do not] count one another's publications or anything like that. It's rather a question of more subtle things. It's a question of how you relate to others in your community and each other's community. Just for example, my husband absolutely refuses to be regarded as [Mary Smith's] husband. (laughter) I'm supposed to be his wife. And for that reason, he doesn't enjoy being in company which is primarily associated with me. . . . And if we have joint acquaintances, as we do, then he's very sort of sensitive to this kind of thing.

(wife's interview)

There is a lot of competition between us which spills over into the rest of our lives. . . . We did some joint work which was very hard on us. . . . That venture just fell apart. . . . A lot of it had to do with a general sense of competition. I probably felt it more than she did for a long time, but she's beginning to feel it, or recognize it. . . . It was difficult to maintain a simple working relationship. . . . And it's difficult in other things too. There are a lot of activities that we go into and whenever we do them together there is a certain amount of difficulty. [Your leisure time activities too?] Not leisure time activities like vacations . . . but involvement in [political] work or this kind of more organized activity that we get in with other groups.   *(husband's interview)*

Given their particular personalities, this couple found it hard to engage in activities together, unless it was something where the woman could fulfill the traditional wifely role; e.g., attend a social gathering primarily associated with the husband's colleagues. Certainly the social setting alone cannot explain the appearance of competitiveness in this couple, since there were other couples who took great pleasure in doing these same kinds of activities. For example, one woman reported that her husband was always particularly proud of her when he attended social gatherings associated with her work and saw the attention and praise she received from her colleagues.

The most commonly used technique for coping with feelings of competition was avoidance. The couple ceased to do that particular activity or get into that particular situation where competitive feelings were apt to be acute. They ceased discussing the aspect of the work that gave them difficulty, they ceased doing joint work, or they ceased attending jointly social gatherings where the wife was apt to receive more attention.

THE TRADITIONAL COUPLES

In the traditional couples, only one member of each marital pair had pursued a career. The lines of achievement of husband and wife were segregated by sex. Therefore, according to proponents of the necessity of such a sex-linked division of labor, competition for status and competitiveness should not have occurred between husband and wife. Furthermore, there should have been no opportunity for other invidious comparisons, feelings of jealousy, or feelings of inferiority to develop. Interviews from the traditional group suggest that there are some flaws in this line of reasoning.

Invidious Comparisons

The experiences of the traditional couples show that a wife, if she places a high value on a career, may feel resentful because she has been relegated to the less prestigious line of achievement; i.e., resentful that she has concentrated so exclusively on family activities which in our society have less prestige than occupational activities. Two of the seven traditional wives did report such invidious comparisons. One wife had been away from her profession for eleven years. In general, she had very much enjoyed this period of domesticity, but when interviewed she was thinking of going back to her profession. She described her feelings as follows:

> I'm very eager and excited at the thought of going back to some activity. . . . I think that I do occasionally feel just a little resentment as to my role as opposed to my husband's role. After all, I make things as easy for him so that he has all the time that he can available for his work. . . . I sometimes wonder a little bit now (laughter) is this fair (laughter) that I should be doing all the work. And although his abilities are greater than mine, maybe I should have a little more time to develop my abilities. But this hasn't bothered me very much. Just once in a while.

She did not think that there would be any professional competitiveness with her husband when she returned to work, because, in her words, he was "ten times more brilliant." She thought, rather, that she might have a "slight inferiority complex" because of his being so much "more advanced and competent." The other woman reported her situation as follows:

> Competition is not the right word. It suggests we're racing. We're too different and in such different fields to be competing. I am intensely envious of the prerogative of a man to devote himself to a career without giving up the family. It is grossly unfair that he should have both. I feel that I can't. I have moments of bitterness about this.

This woman felt obligated to spend considerable time serving the family, and she had made many more sacrifices for her husband's career than vice versa. As the quote shows, there were times when she resented it.[12] The fact that this woman thinks a man can devote himself to a career without giving up the family is, incidentally, her perception of the situation. In actuality, many men who devote themselves to a career "have" a family only in the minimal sense. It exists, but the men participate very little in family activities. In an emotional sense, such men have "given up" the family, but, of course, this is different from the issue of how the situation is perceived.

These two women, strictly speaking, were not bothered by feelings of competitiveness. But certainly the comparisons they made vis-à-vis their husbands were invidious. They expressed resentment or envy over the fact that they "had not been allowed to play the game." They had been unable to enter the occupational world on anything even remotely approaching a basis of equality of opportunity with their husbands. These two women both saw value in having a career and saw occupational pursuits as being worthwhile. Yet they had spent a considerable portion of their life primarily serving the husband and family. Both these women had, since marriage, primarily arranged their lives for the benefit of the husband's career. Since they did have some desire to pursue their own profession, they saw their situation as less favorable than that of their husband. This is in contrast to several other comparison women who also primarily arranged their lives to serve the husband, but who did not have any strong interest in a career of their own. In these latter cases, the women readily accepted the role of server and did not make resentful comments about their position.

Competitiveness: Why Not?

The traditional couples — women and men — said that they had not experienced a sense of competition when the wife worked and did not think it would be a problem if the wife returned to work in the future. The sole exception was one husband: he thought that the wife's former work had caused a slight amount of competitiveness early in their marriage.

Objectively competitiveness did not correlate with what activities the husband and wife engaged in, but when the traditional couples were asked what prevented competitiveness, they, like the professional couples, cited a dissimilarity of activities as the reason. In other words, when competitiveness did not occur the traditional couples also had their own perceived explanations of what prevented it. Most often they said it did not occur because the marital partners did different things. In some cases, this explanation was like that given by the professional group. Doing different things meant that they were in different fields, worked for different employers, or had different skills. However, some traditional couples said explicitly that they meant they had different roles. They said the wife was primarily a wife and any work she did was ancillary. The husband was defined as *the* breadwinner and as "operating on a different level." For example, one wife described how it was very explicit in their household thát the husband was the breadwinner and that her work did "not encroach on his responsibility as a father and the head of the household." In another couple the wife explained, as follows, why competitiveness had not occurred:

> *Because he's just smarter than I am (laughter). . . . I never took a career that seriously and I do think that his career is important. And we're just not operating on the same level.*

The husband's explanation agreed with hers. He said that she played a different role. Even in non-work areas, the two of them operated on different levels. He said:

> *It's a different kind of role that she plays. . . . She's very active in local communal affairs, and I'm active in certain national problems, so I don't see this as any kind of competition or threat. She can run [the local community] and I'll run Washington. This is how we generally define it.*

The other perceived explanation, among the comparison group, for lack of competitiveness was that the husband was more successful than the wife or that he was "more brilliant."

CONCLUSION

The present study has suggested a departure from the theories which stress the necessity of a sex-linked division of labor, and which predict that the pursuit of careers by marital partners would result in competitive feelings between them. These theories assume the following: 1) Presently the sexes are not engaged "in a race." 2) Feelings of competition and invidious comparison are eliminated when sex roles are segregated, but will exist when the sex roles are not segregated; thus the central issue is segregated vs. non-segregated roles. 3) It is a norm that marital partners be equal in status. 4) The realm where they would compete is the occupational realm.

In contrast, the analysis presented in this chapter starts by recognizing that our society now equates masculinity with superiority. It thus assumes the following: 1) The sexes are already engaged in a race. 2) The issue of segregated vs. non-segregated sex roles is irrelevant as regards the presence or absence of competitive feelings and invidious comparisons. 3) The current norm is that the husband should be superior to the wife. 4) Competitive feelings, if they exist, can occur in any type of activity. The central issue is that the cultural norm now dictates the husband should be superior to his wife — in any activity he wishes to be good at, not just work.

NOTES

1. Talcott Parsons, "The Kinship System of the Contemporary United States," *Essays in Sociological Theory* (rev. ed.; New York: Free Press, 1954), p. 192. (Emphasis in the original.) For additional statements of how Parsons sees segregated sex roles as functional for the solidarity of the family see: Talcott Parsons, "An Analytical Approach to the Theory of Social Stratification," *Essays,* p. 79; Talcott Parsons, "Age and Sex in the Social Structure of the United States," *Essays,* (footnote) p. 94; and, Talcott Parsons, "The Social Structure of the Family," *The Family: Its Function and Destiny,* ed. Ruth Nanda Anshen (New York: Harper, 1949), pp. 193-95.

2. Parsons, "Kinship System," p. 192.

3. Robert E. Park and Ernest W. Burgess, *Introduction to the Science of Sociology* (Chicago: University of Chicago Press, 1921), p. 709. More recently a similar distinction was made by Jessie Bernard when she observed that "the concepts 'competitiveness' and 'level of aspiration' are social-psychological rather than, strictly speaking, sociological concepts. People may be 'in competition' with one another without being at all 'competitive.' " Jessie Bernard, *Academic Women* (New York: World Publishing Co., 1966), p. 308. (First published 1964: Pennsylvania State University.) See also Jessie Bernard, *American Community Behavior* (rev. ed., New York: Holt, Rinehart and Winston, 1962), p. 66.

4. Marya Mannes, "The Problems of Creative Women," *The Potential of Woman,* eds. Seymour M. Farber and Roger H. L. Wilson (New York: McGraw-Hill, 1963), p. 127.

5. Matina S. Horner, "Woman's Will To Fail," *Psychology Today* (Nov., 1969), p. 38.

6. Anon., "Jean-Claude Killy and The Winter Woman," *Ladies' Home Journal* (November, 1969), p. 87.

7. Lipsyte's amusing spoof is only a slight exaggeration of what the opposing players said during TV coverage of the event. Robert Lipsyte, "Sports of the Times: The Florence League," *New York Times,* August 20, 1970, p. 45. See also *Life* (August 28, 1970).

8. Cynthia Fuchs Epstein, "Women and Professional Careers: The Case of the Woman Lawyer" (unpublished Ph.D. dissertation, Columbia University, 1968), p. 210. (Emphasis in the original.)

9. *Ibid.,* pp. 213-14.

10. I would like to thank Philip E. Slater for discussions which helped clarify the issues involved in analyzing competitiveness between the sexes.

11. The fact that an occasional couple can adjust to the wife's superior achievement is very important in showing that in some cases it is possible to do so. Nevertheless, it is still predicted that at present many people would experience this as a problem.

12. An interesting case study of a housewife feeling resentful and making invidious comparisons is presented in a book by Bernard. The woman had

been a housewife for almost sixteen years before returning to preparation for a career. "I was definitely career-oriented when I was young. . . . [But] I had not gotten launched on a career by the time I was married. . . . His work took him all over the world. While he was becoming ever more of a cosmopolite, I was becoming more and more parochial. I hated it. . . . I didn't feel the way a satisfied housewife should feel. . . . I felt trapped and resentful and blamed my husband for much of it. I was jealous of his freedom. I envied him his trips abroad, and sometimes I wasn't a very good sport about it." Bernard, *Academic Women*, pp. 228-30.

8

Colleagueship

*We always edit each other's stuff.
. . Everything I've written she's
read. And everything she's written
I've read.*
Husband, professional couple

*There was a feeling of frustration
on her part when I talked about
technical aspects. . . . She knew
how to do that once and . . . she
hadn't kept up.*
Husband, traditional couple

People usually do not get married in order to be professional colleagues
with each other. A colleague relationship and a marriage relationship
are supposed to fulfill different needs in a person's life. And in the normal course of events, one usually has these two types of relationships
with different people rather than with the same person. Yet when both
marital partners have careers, the possibility exists that they will also
be colleagues. If so, it adds a new dimension to the marriage. It is
something that really is not possible if only one spouse has a profession. If it occurs, it is a positive aspect of the two-career family which
can offset many of the problems discussed previously.

Mutual conversation and shared interests are part of the middle-
class marital pattern even if the wife is not employed.[1] In addition to
general conversation, there is often discussion specifically of work —
or at least a monologue of the husband's job woes. One thinks, for
example, of how corporation wives have been described as "sounding
boards" and "wailing walls."[2] In such cases the discussion of work
is primarily one-way, with the husband explaining or complaining to
his wife. When the wife also has a career, the question is whether she

121

discusses her occupational problems with her husband. In the two-career family where both spouses are intellectually competent and professionally trained, do the husband and wife in addition discuss the type of problem that they might discuss with colleagues? Do they influence each other intellectually? Do they make suggestions or collaborate? If they do, what happens to them personally? What happens when a relationship which was designed for one purpose gets used for some other purpose? Is it actually possible for a marital relationship to be also a colleague relationship?

DISCUSSION OF WORK

Almost all the professional couples, specifically nineteen of the twenty, said they discussed various aspects of the wife's work. Common topics of discussion were interpersonal relationships and general professional issues; for example, administrative relationships, financing of research, scientific news of general interest, meetings, grants, and professional policy. One husband explained:

> We discuss things, you know, and I know what she's doing. . . . We do have a good deal of conversation about particular individuals, individual scholars, types of scholarship, how good this, that, and the other thing is — not to mention all the business of colleges, which we're both very interested in.

There was only one couple that hardly discussed the wife's work at all. This couple occasionally discussed some peripheral aspect of the job, such as mutual acquaintances. But in this case, the husband and wife both stressed that neither her work nor his work was a strong mutual interest.

Almost all the professional couples, specifically eighteen of the twenty, also reported that they discussed the actual content of the wife's work. One woman described the discussions as follows:

> I tell him what I'm doing (laughter) or what I plan to do; he tells me what he's doing, what he plans to do. I don't understand much of what he's doing [in science]; it's a little esoteric unless you're a specialist in the field. My work? He says he understands it more because it's more within the canon of everybody to understand.

There was variation in the depth with which couples discussed the content of the wife's work. At least a third of those who discussed the content, said they did so only in "superficial terms" or only in laymen's language; these were all couples in which the spouses were in very different fields.

The findings regarding the opposite question — whether they discussed the husband's work — are quite similar. Almost all, specifically nineteen of the twenty, discussed some aspects of the husband's work, such as interpersonal relationships and general professional issues. Most couples, specifically sixteen of the twenty, also discussed the actual content of the husband's work. At least a third of these said they discussed the content only in superficial terms or laymen's language.

The most common reason given for lack of discussion or for superficial discussion was the inability to understand the other's specialized field. The couples' comments reflect the degree to which fields of professional activity are specialized today. In no case did one spouse have a deep understanding of the content of the other spouse's work when they were in non-related fields, even when the spouse was in a humanities or social science field generally thought to be quite accessible to lay audiences. Unless in the same or related fields, most of the individuals discussed their spouse's work only "until it got technical" or "until it went into details and subtleties." One woman, who was in a different scientific field than her husband, explained as follows:

> [Do you talk about the content of your work?] Oh, sure, up to a point. But you know, I can't follow him into the far realms of mathematics, and he isn't sufficiently knowledgeable to understand all the subtleties of some of the things I am doing. And it would require so long to get caught up. The kind of thing that we're more apt to discuss are other people's papers, for instance, that are new breakthroughs in aspects [of his field or of my field]. Bits of scientific news, and this kind of thing.

And even a woman who was in a field of humanities typically considered part of a general education felt her husband did not understand the subtleties. She said, "I think the finer points he doesn't understand, and I don't expect him to. I mean when I get excited about having discovered some little bit of data hidden in a document it doesn't really stir him, and I know it."

Lack of time was also cited by some as a reason for not discussing the content of the spouse's work more. A few mentioned the problem of time in connection with the problem of specialized knowledge; even if one was interested in learning the spouse's specialty, it would be impractical to do so in terms of the amount of time it would require. For example, one woman explained by saying, "I make no effort to know [his field] at his level. I don't have the time to do it. Neither of us tries to run two professional lives to assist the other." Furthermore, even a few couples who were already in the same field and who had done collaborative work also mentioned the pressures of time. One woman explained:

> Well I know what he's doing and he knows what I'm doing on those areas that are outside [of our joint work]. We don't get that much time to talk to each other. I mean, there's 24 hours in a day and that's not so much. We have lots of things going on.

There were a few couples out of the twenty who refrained from discussing the content of their work as a way of compartmentalizing their life. They found it easier in terms of their personalities and their relationship to keep the two careers separate in this way. Two couples had done this throughout their married life. And there was also a couple in which the husband and wife had more recently adopted the technique. They had begun to avoid discussion of a certain content area because it was during such discussion that their feelings of competitiveness became more acute. The husband explained:

> My wife has discussed her work with me in the past. After our attempt to work together, there has been a good deal less discussion than there was before. . . . I'd say now we really don't discuss her work to the extent that we discuss mine.

He thought that this arrangement was part of "an ongoing conflict . . . about working together and competition."

DISCUSSION AS COLLEAGUES

Almost all people in professional couples, as reported above, did discuss some aspect of their work with their spouses. This is not surprising, given the prevalent expectation in our society that the spouse's role, especially the wife's, is to be one of nurturing the marital partner's ego. This requires listening and giving sympathetic understanding.

What is more questionable is whether current expectations also include the idea of there being a genuine dialogue between husband and wife on professional matters — a dialogue involving independent suggestions and professional criticism. Yet if both spouses are professionally trained and discuss work, independent suggestions probably will be made — either on the content of the spouse's work, how to handle administrative issues, or on questions of style.

Can a relationship primarily based on marriage also become one of colleagueship? Can marital partners discuss intellectual things in a manner detached enough so that intellectual disagreements are not meant to be, and are not perceived to be, personal affronts? This issue is raised by the case studies presented in a recent study of academic women. In one case, for example, the wife describes how at first collaboration between spouses meant mutual criticism sessions which were hard on both of them; only later did they come to learn the difference between making debating points and having a cooperative discussion.[3]

In the present study, most professional couples said they were able to discuss work without being "too personal" about it. Specifically, slightly over two thirds of the couples said they were able to discuss the wife's or the husband's work without the discussion leading to any "personal argument." This does not mean that they completely agreed on everything, but rather that a difference of opinion was not taken as a personal affront. In other words, in the context of the interview, the aim was to get some sense of the emotional tone of such discussions. The issue was not whether they ever had a difference of opinion or a disagreement. The issue was whether such disagreements, if they occurred, came to be colored with personal feelings and experienced as painful.

Some couples, in addition, even reported being able to give and accept criticism without there being feelings of resentment. For example, one woman who gave some of her work to her husband for criticism, explained as follows how this did not cause problems for them:

> *I asked him to. And I suppose when I ask someone to read something and criticize I really want the criticism because that's what can be most helpful. And it's been up to me either to accept or reject what he said. I don't think either of us felt personal about this at all.*

Less than a third of the professional couples reported that discussions over work led to personal arguments between them. Only three couples out of the twenty reported severe difficulties in this respect, and they were couples who also reported experiencing feelings of competitiveness. In these couples, it was particular types of discussion over work that were taken personally, while other professional topics were still discussed with equanimity. For example, one couple experienced personal arguments especially when they tried to do joint work. As the husband explained, working together became like the classic case of married people trying to teach each other how to drive. "It was diffi-

cult to maintain a simple working relationship while doing this together." As a result, they ceased to do joint work.

In another couple discussions were taken personally only when they
involved the editing of each other's work. Their solution was to continue extensive editing of each other's work, but to write out the comments rather than discuss them face-to-face. The husband explained:

> *What we used to do was read over it together and tell each other and that
> was very tough because neither one liked to be criticized. So what we do
> is write out our comments now. Then we can each read what the other
> one has to say in a cool, calm atmosphere and it works out perfectly that
> way. . . . [But] it used to really be violent because nobody likes to be told,
> "Well this doesn't make sense." It didn't, but I mean it was hard to be
> told that. If you read it (laughter), it becomes impersonal.*

As can be seen, the main technique these couples used for dealing
with personal arguments over work was avoidance. They avoided
discussion of those topics that led to personal argument, although they
continued to discuss other aspects of their work.

INFLUENCE ON EACH OTHER'S WORK

With two highly trained people in one family, the possibility exists
that they will influence each other's thinking, even though they may
not have an intimate knowledge of each other's field. If the two spouses
are in the same field, they are by definition qualified to comment as a
colleague might. If they are in different fields, there is the opportunity
for learning about aspects of another profession with which one might
not ordinarily become acquainted. Then possibilities exist for inte-
grating concepts from the two disciplines.

Most people in the professional group gave examples of ways their
work was influenced by their marital partner. Sometimes this influence
was minor, sometimes major. Half the women and over a third of the
men gave examples of how their spouse had influenced their work in
ways which might be classified as relatively minor; for example, editing the other person's work for style, clarity, and logic; suggesting
ways in which the thinking could be more rigorous and organized; and
suggesting various references with which the spouse might not be
familiar. At the least, such "minor" influence meant some suggestions
on style; for example, one woman said her husband had a very good
command of language and that she expressed things more clearly because of discussions with him. At the most, it meant extensive editing

which included comments on the ideas. In one couple where editing did extend to a discussion of the ideas, the husband commented as follows on their mutual influence.

> *We always edit each other's stuff. . . . If I say something that's either poorly written or there are logical inconsistencies, it's changed right away. Everything I've written she's read. And everything she's written I've read. And in her book, she lacked a conclusion, so I suggested a conclusion for her. And she's done similar things for me.*

This couple said that their fields were too different to ever publish anything together; but, there was enough overlap so that they could understand each other's ideas and comment on them.

More "major ways" in which the spouse had influenced their work were described by seven women and also by seven men. They said, for example, that through the spouse they were able to see another aspect or side of the problem, another view of the issue, another approach. The spouses acquainted them with new topics, or the subjects on which they chose to do research were influenced by the interests of the spouse. In six cases such influence was symmetrical — it went in both directions. For example, in one couple in the same field the husband and wife said they had a tendency to work on problems they could do together. The wife explained that there were some problems that neither one of them would have done individually, but together it made a lot of sense to try them. Although in the same field, they had different individual styles and thought they could complement one another by doing joint work. In another couple the husband and wife were in different fields, but they both were influenced by the research interests of the other. Although never publishing jointly, each ended up doing some borderline work which was unusual for a person in their own discipline. The husband explained:

> *I have tended to do work which is close to hers, and she has tended to do some work which is close to mine, which probably wouldn't have happened if we hadn't been married. I did a long interview series, some of the questions of which clearly stemmed from her interests. . . . One whole chapter in the book turned out to be fundamentally related to this. And I doubt that I would have gotten interested in this or would have known anything about it because . . . it's not the sort of thing [a person in my field] usually knows much about or is very much interested in.*

He gave a complementary example showing how his interests had influenced her; she in turn built on the results of his study, and followed up a topic that was unusual for someone in her discipline. In this case two careers in one family clearly contributed to the merging of two fields of study.

A few of the people mentioned how the spouse had influenced some other aspect of their work, such as handling interpersonal relationships, carrying out some administrative procedure, instituting a policy reform. For example, one man's employer had accepted a suggestion of his on how to recruit more minority group members, and the man explained that actually he had originally gotten the idea from his wife. There were only a few people who gave no indication of having been influenced intellectually by their spouse at all. A few people contradicted themselves, saying that they had not been influenced, but yet giving some examples of how they were influenced. For example, one woman said:

> Very frequently he will suggest reading that I am unfamiliar with. That will go into the work, and it would not have without him. . . . I don't think he influences my thinking.

Such people were counted, in the analysis above, as having been influenced by the marital partner.

So far only the obvious ways in which spouses influence each other intellectually have been mentioned — overtly through discussion, suggesting references, and doing joint work. The influence may occur through more subtle processes as well. It undoubtedly occurs through many ways in which the people are not aware of themselves—through general discussions they hardly remember, through what books are in the home, through what people their spouse introduces them to. One woman was particularly interesting in this respect. She described how she was drawn, through her husband, more toward *his* colleagues than toward her own. In a way that is highly atypical among the professional women, she began to be very deeply influenced by what they thought and even by how they used certain concepts. Her comments are particularly interesting in that they illustrate, as she said, "the invisibles" by which one's thinking may be influenced.

> It's not really so much whether I discuss my work with my husband. . . . But whom do I see? Who are the professional people that I have the most contact with? . . . The problems that I see, not consciously, but the problems that I literally perceive are very deeply influenced by the style of perception of [people in my husband's field]. And I am sure that my work is very much influenced by this. . . . My conclusions — I'm deeply influenced by what [his colleagues] think important. So, you see, what you have there is far more than the problem of do I talk about my work with my husband. That question is, I think, offensive in its simplemindedness.

That is not the way it works. It works through more invisibles than that. And I would think one of the key factors in this is simply through your husband into what circle of people are you drawn — because it's clear that that is the pull that is very strong.

JOINT WORK

Perhaps the ultimate test of colleagueship among marriage partners is whether they can do joint work if they so desire. Can they work together on the same project? Here there would seem to be no way to avoid discussion of the content of one's work, no way to keep conversations of work at an anecdotal level, and no way to completely segregate the two careers from each other or from the marriage relationship.[4]

Among the twenty professional couples, three had successfully and enjoyably done joint work for many years. However, not all of their work was done together; within each of these three couples, the husband and the wife also did separate projects too. One other couple had briefly tried joint work, but they found it so painful that they gave it up. This was the couple that had had the greatest problems with competitiveness. Their feelings of competitiveness had been especially acute when they discussed work and when they tried to work together.

Couples were asked to explain how they went about doing joint work. In all three cases where such work went well, their descriptions were very similar. They said that one spouse did one part of a problem better, and that the other spouse did another part of the problem better. They defined themselves as being complementary. One wife explained as follows:

> *Over the years we've worked very effectively together. . . . The way this thing works out in working together is that we complement each other. We're good at different parts of the problem, and that's what's made it a good team. He likes my contribution and when I can't work with him on a problem and he's worked with other people he's complained because he's gotten so used to me, and vice versa. . . . It's not so much competition because we don't really work on the same parts of the problem . . . but we work in parallel. We work at different aspects of it and then compare notes. . . . We've been working together nearly ten years. . . . We've worked a lot of problems together by now.*

In the end it might be difficult to say who did what because each person went over and made some suggestions regarding the other person's contribution. But, nevertheless, each person tended to accept the other person's special competence for some part of the work. Rather than define the situation in competitive terms — each trying to outdo the other on every point — they defined it in complementary terms. This outlook was missing in the couple whose attempt to do joint work was unsuccessful.

THE TRADITIONAL COUPLES

The traditional couples, in general, were less apt to discuss their work with each other as colleagues. Because of the way people were selected for the study, some traditional women no longer had work to discuss. Those traditional women who eventually had returned to their professions part time said they did discuss certain aspects of their work with their husbands, such as interpersonal relationships and substantive aspects that they thought were of general interest. Most traditional husbands said they discussed "personalities" and interpersonal relations with their wives, such as how to get along with colleagues, staffing problems, what to do if a secretary was unsatisfactory. Regarding the content of their work, most traditional husbands felt that their wives could not appreciate the "technical details." This view is quite similar to that of many professional couples where one spouse could not understand the technical details of another field, even though both did have careers. However, among the traditional group, two of the seven husbands went on to comment that they felt their wives were less informed or could understand less now that they were no longer working. For example, one husband said that previously his wife had been a better theoretician than he had been. But he no longer discussed technical things with her because she could not follow it. He explained:

> [There] was a feeling of frustration on her part when I talked about technical aspects because she was once, of course, completely up-to-date on all that stuff. As she got away from it, why it would and did produce feelings of intense frustration because she knew how to do that once and she didn't know anymore or she hadn't kept up.

Another man felt that since his wife had been "cooped up" in the house for so long, she "didn't have the scope she had before."

Influences between husband and wife on their work were less apparent in the traditional group. The influences that did occur — with only one exception — were the "minor type" such as commenting on style. Or they sometimes made suggestions on how to handle an interpersonal relationship. For example, one woman said she sometimes read a report for her husband just to see if it made sense. She explained:

> Occasionally he has brought home reports and asked me to read them. And I know there have been a couple where I found certain sections unclear, that I haven't understood. And he's decided that if I can't understand it, then he probably ought to rewrite it.

Another traditional woman mentioned influencing only her husband's relationships with people. She said, "I haven't influenced his work at all, but I have influenced his relationships with co-workers."

There was only one traditional couple in which the wife had had a "major" influence on the husband's work. This influence occurred early in their relationship. They had been students together. The husband explained how helpful she had been in getting his doctoral dissertation done. He himself was an experimentalist; and she had been a theoretician. He explained her influence:

> [She] was of tremendous help in getting [the thesis] done, I must say. Not only from the point of view of motivation, but also helping explain the theory to me. . . . The theory that we were using — or that she was teaching me — was a theory closely related to the stuff she was doing. And as I say, she's a much sharper theoretician than I am.

This kind of influence did not continue later. By the time of the interview, the wife had been out of the labor force for many years, and she had not kept up on technical matters.

When asked about their influence on the husband's work, the traditional women sometimes answered more "as a wife" than "as a colleague." Three of the seven answered from such a point of view. They talked of influencing the husband's work by entertaining for him or by giving him emotional support. One woman responded as follows:

> [Do you think you have influenced the content or style of his work?] Well now, it depends. If you mean his real work, no. If you mean the style, for example in which he entertains his staff, that sort of thing, yes. But not the real meat of his work.

Another traditional wife thought she had influenced her husband because with her support he was more willing to tackle a difficult job. She said:

> Well I would say our marriage was probably related to his ability to tackle a much more tasking job. He is more enthusiastic about going to meetings if I go along.

At meetings she could act as a buffer between him and the demands of his business associates. In these situations, the wife consistently played the subordinate role. She promoted the husband's career by doing ancillary activities rather than by collaborating or commenting as a colleague might.

NOTES

1. They are components of the joint conjugal role-relationship described by Bott. Elizabeth Bott, *Family and Social Network* (London: Tavistock Publications, 1957).

2. William H. Whyte, Jr., "The Wives of Management," *Man, Work, and Society*, ed. Sigmund Nosow and William H. Form (New York: Basic Books, 1962), p. 549. (First published in 1951: *Fortune*.)

3. Jessie Bernard, *Academic Women* (New York: World Publishing Co., 1966), pp. 234-35. (First published in 1964: Pennsylvania State University.)

4. Here joint work refers to projects which were done together as colleagues. It does not refer to other forms of collaboration; for example, to a situation where the wife plays a more traditional role by being the husband's research assistant or silent editor.

9

The Male View

*Her work is pretty good — and
shall I say it? — damn good. . . .
She's a highly competent professional person.*
Husband, professional couple

*Her return to work has been cast as
an ancillary activity. . . . It's just
giving her an outlet.*
Husband, traditional couple

How does the husband view the wife's career? His attitude, it was predicted, would be one of the most important factors regarding the outcome of an attempt to have a two-career family. If the husband did not
approve of the second career, he probably would not be willing to help
make it possible. It is not possible for a wife to follow a serious profession and yet have the husband's life remain exactly as it would be
if she were a housewife. The husband has to be willing to make some
changes in his own life.

To swim against the tide may take considerable determination. To
provide one's own individual solutions — because the society does
not make solutions to the problems of the two-career family widely
available — may require considerable effort. In this connection, it
was thought that the husband's attitude — positive, ambivalent, or
negative — would be important in at least two ways. It would influence the degree to which the husband would encourage his wife to
believe that she was indeed justified in pursuing her profession and
being an atypical wife. Moreover, it would influence the degree to
which he was willing to put up with the other changes which seem to
be concomitant with a second career in the family.

The emphasis here on the importance of the husband's attitude and actions is in keeping with several other studies of women's careers which have also cited this as a crucial factor. Information collected recently from female dentists, business executives, physicians, and academicians shows that women in all these fields see the husband's attitude as important.[1] Thus, "whatever plans are made for the recruitment of women — and this would hold for any learned profession — must of necessity include men. The preparation of men is as intrinsic a part of preparation for women's careers as that of the women themselves."[2] As the results presented below show, the present study confirms the usefulness of looking at the male view.

THE HUSBAND'S ATTITUDE

In almost all professional couples, the husband was very supportive of the wife's career. This was so according both to the wife's report and the husband's report. When asked about the husband's attitude, the women said things like "he has encouraged me and helped me in every way." "He applauds and he supports my career." "He is my main souce of encouragement." One woman spoke as follows:

> I have been extremely fortunate in having a husband who has been more than willing to help me, to make it possible for me to pursue my own interests, my own professional interests. . . . When I wanted to apply for [a grant to study abroad], he said fine, it was only fair that I should have that opportunity.

In no professional couple was the husband's view negative. However, among the twenty, there were two cases where the wife reported that her husband's attitude was mixed. These two said that on the conscious, rational level, the husband was in favor of the wife career, but there were subterranean emotional reservations. As one explained, "he is intellectually committed to my working, but that doesn't mean committed in every way at all times. And there certainly have been run-ins on that." These two couples were also atypical in other ways. In one such case the wife had worked less than any of the other professional wives. The other such case was the couple which manifested the most conflict and competitiveness over the two careers.

The interviews with the husbands of the professional wives revealed, in almost all cases, very favorable attitudes toward the wife's career. They said things like "I think women have to have interests other than the home." "I want her to have a career." "I try to advance her career whenever I can." Occasionally a husband even gave a polemical reply — a statement pro women's rights. For example, one husband said that after seeing the problems his wife faced, he had developed some very strong views. He was very critical of the prevailing attitude in this country that a "woman's place is in the home." He said:

> As I say, there's a kind of state of mind. I can find it among graduate students and everybody else. Male students who are very liberal in most everything are not particularly liberal on these questions. There still is this old attitude. . . . This culture demands that women stay home though I get the impression that a large number of women get bored to death at it.

He said he had done "some preaching" on the subject. He also had encouraged certain female graduate students to continue with their careers despite the prevailing opinion about women.

The husband's general attitude toward the wife's career only tells part of the story. Several more subtle aspects emerged from the interviews. First of all, it became apparent that most of these husbands took their wives' work seriously — in the sense of respecting it. This was most apparent in the interviews with the husbands themselves. Many indicated that they were proud of their wives' accomplishments or that they regarded their wives as competent professionals. One spoke as follows:

> Her work is pretty good — and shall I say it? — damn good. She produced a book last year and has another book in press right now. . . . For my money, she's a highly competent professional person and deserves every opportunity to fulfill herself.

Other husbands explained what creative contributions the wife had made, referred to the wife as a prominent professional, or said that the wife did superb research and was a real scholar. The intellectual influences between husband and wife — analyzed in the previous chapter — would be another example of respect for the wife's abilities. And also, almost all husbands in the professional group thought of the wife's career as a "life-long goal," rather than merely "something to keep her occupied."

Secondly, in slightly over half these couples, at least one partner mentioned that the husband wanted the wife "to be happy" or "to be the kind of person she was" — and that involved having a career. As one woman explained:

> You know very well that if you didn't [have a career] you probably would be a hellion to live with because you'd be so unhappy and so resentful. . . . And my husband says, "You go right ahead and do what's going to

> *make you happy because if you're happy then I'll be happy, and the house will be a more pleasant place to live in."*

And in another couple, the man — one of the few with mixed attitudes toward the wife's career — saw what the paradox would be of asking her to quit:

> *If I want my wife to be the person that she is, this [career] is an absolutely necessary part of her life. That's just the way she is. And it contributes to the qualities that I like in her.*

He saw that there would be advantages if she were at home more, but he also saw that career involvement was such an integral part of her personality, that to confine her at home "would turn her into a different person."

Thirdly, when asked how the husband felt about a wife's career which involved a great deal of time, energy, and emotion, most couples reported that the husband did not object. In a few couples the husband even felt the wife should be more involved than she was. One man explained why he felt this way:

> *It's very difficult to make an effective and successful career . . . without a great deal of effort and really unconscionable hours and energy and single-minded devotion. . . . I think she sometimes feels more relaxed about it, maybe less compulsive than I am . . . and at the same time she is disappointed.*

From time to time he would tell his wife that she had to work harder if she wanted to keep up with the competition. Yet these replies should not obscure the fact that elsewhere in the interview some people mentioned that it would be nice if the wife were more available to the husband in terms of time.

Husbands in the professional group not only had positive attitudes toward the wife's career. Even more importantly, they translated their approval into concrete, practical acts of support. Almost all were willing to alter their own behavior and change their own way of life so as to make two careers in one family a reality. The previous chapters have already given abundant evidence of this. The husbands in two-career families, relative to those in the traditional group, were more apt to take the wife's career needs into account when moving, more willing to help with domestic and child-rearing duties, and more willing to take the wife into consideration when setting up their time schedules.

In addition, many husbands in two-career families helped their wives in other ways. For example, one husband taught the wife's classes the first week after she had a baby. Another made the original suggestion that the wife apply to graduate school. A third waged a battle on the wife's behalf to get a rule regarding women's employment changed. Still another fended off outside criticism of the wife's career by standing up for "their way of life."

The husbands in professional couples either actively helped their wives, or at a bare minimum, did not complain very much about any inconvenience that their careers might cause. In most couples, the wife did not feel that the husband set up conflicting expectations — such as wanting her to have a career but expecting the house always to be perfect and the dinner always on time.

BE CAREFUL WHO YOU MARRY

Almost all the professional women stressed the *importance* of the husband's attitude and help. They perceived the husband's support as being crucial. They said things like "the choice of a husband is very important in making a career possible — if you don't have a husband that supports you and is interested in your work, you can't survive." "You've got to have a *very* understanding husband." "This really is the secret — to be careful who you marry."

Two thirds of the women thought the husband's attitude so crucial that they mentioned its importance spontaneously. They either emphasized the issue even before they were asked about it, or later in the interview they returned of their own accord to the topic to stress it. Following is a quote from one such woman:

> I might say in general that my present husband has the best attitude towards my working that a husband possibly could. And I try to impress it on my own students that if you're going to combine working with marriage, you have got to have a husband not who tolerates this, but who actively wants you to work. Because, you know, the toleration will go just so far. But when you're up against it and you need help and support, then you've got to have this from a husband who wants you to do what you're doing, rather than putting up with it.

The women who spontaneously brought up the importance of the husband's attitude did so in connection with the following issues: how they were able to get both career and home responsibilities done (e.g., how they could leave home for professional travel); how the husband overlooked certain inconveniences due to the wife's career (e.g., a hectic time schedule); what advice they gave to their students who asked about careers for women; or what they thought it was important to stress most in the overall interview.

The tremendous importance of the husband's attitude, however, does not mean that the women were passive in the process. They played an active role in the outcome too. For example, several professional women were willing to marry only men who had favorable attitudes toward career wives. And of the twenty professional women, two divorced a prior husband who was not supportive of their career — giving up the marriage rather than giving up the career. Thus, it is not accurate to say the husband's attitude must be favorable for a wife to continue her career. It is more accurate to say the husband's attitude must be favorable for her to *combine* marriage and career, within the context of any given marriage.

In most professional couples, the wife's and the husband's expectations and actions had a mutually reinforcing effect. The wife, at some point in time, became committed to her career. The husband approved. And the importance of her career as well as his seems to have become a basic assumption for both of them. Evidence for this statement comes from both an overall assessment of the interviews, as well as from specific comments. For example, one husband said — in explaining a decision they had made — "it was all part of the program"; that is, part of the program to make two careers possible. In another couple, the husband in trying to think of what it would be like if the wife did not work, said he just could not imagine that kind of life. And in response to whether he minded his wife's great involvement in a career, another man said, "This has gone on ever since we were married and I never thought of it any other way."

PERCEIVED EFFECTS OF THE SECOND CAREER

There are many paradoxical interrelations between the professional commitments of husband and wife, as should be clear from the previous chapters. Each partner's career simultaneously may help and hinder the other partner's career. How these paradoxes are perceived by a person is a somewhat different question, and one that was pursued in connection with the husband's attitude.

Most husbands said they had not felt hindered by the wife's career. A few said that, had they been married to some other woman, they probably would have had a different career, either in terms of where they moved or what topics they studied; but they further said that one had no way of knowing whether this would have been better. No husband in the professional group stressed solely the negative aspects of the wife's career. The few men who thought it had had drawbacks, also mentioned its advantages. For example, one man thought that if his wife did not work, she could be the perfect secretary for him; yet he also felt that he would not be happy living with that kind of woman. He explained:

> Of course there is the man whose wife at home would be something like his secretary also. Well, that would help. But I know — with absolute evidence — that I would be at the same time very unhappy. She would type for me or look in the library for the things I would indicate — make the sacrifice of being the perfect secretary. But I would resent it. . . . I feel more comfortable [the way it is] — where there is the possibility of dialogue and companionship too. That is greatly appreciated.

Another man listed as drawbacks the fact that one move had been influenced by the wife, and also the fact that he could not follow the time-saving practice of his colleagues who were able to turn all family management — planning trip itineraries, the checkbook, the taxes — over to a non-working wife. As advantages, he listed the fact that her contacts, knowledge, and interest had been a positive influence on his research and writing. Finally, he felt that he was better off having a wife who could be a critic rather than having a highly doting and worshipping wife whose whole life was wrapped up in her husband's career.

Many husbands mentioned some way in which they felt the wife's career had helped them. However, in specifying the advantage, they did not necessarily distinguish between something due to her career *per se*, and something due to her personality or their relationship. Some said the wife's career was an asset for a reason directly related to her profession; for example, the specific knowledge she had was useful to them. Some mentioned her general intelligence and personality, or suggested that having a career made her the kind of person they could really talk to. A few simply thought they were better off because they had a good marital relationship.

Husbands were not only asked about the perceived effect of the wife's career on "big issues" such as on their own overall careers. They were also asked about the perceived effect on "little issues" and "everyday tensions." What happened if only one car was available and they both needed it to get to work? What happened if someone was late for dinner because of work? Husbands in the professional group — with only one exception — did not cite such events as chronic issues related to the wife's career. Most often they answered to the effect that "things like a dilemma over the car do occur, but they're not an issue." They made comments like, "Oh sure, [they happen] but we cope." "This happens, but it is no issue — we both get to work somehow." "We both go home late and it would be nice if supper was there, but we don't think about that. . . . All of these things we take in our stride." A few husbands did cite some chronic issue or complaint — such as bad cooking or perpetual tardiness — but thought it would occur whether the wife worked or did not work. In only one case did the husband report these everyday events as a focal point of conflict and blame the conflict on the wife's career. This was in the couple which had experienced the most competitiveness and the most conflict specifically related to two careers. The implication would seem to be that it is not the presence or absence of an event itself — such as tardiness — which is crucial. Rather, any minor event can serve as a focal point for conflict caused by some other aspect of the people's lives.

THE TRADITIONAL COUPLES

Traditional husbands were less likely to have favorable attitudes toward a career for the wife than were husbands in the professional group. This was so both according to the wife's report and the husband's report. Half the traditional husbands were opposed to such careers and saw only part-time work or an "eventual" return to work as acceptable. Half, however, did express favorable attitudes toward a career for the wife.

The professional and traditional couples differed on subtle aspects of the husband's attitude even more than they did on the general category "husband in favor of wife's career" vs. "husband opposed." First of all, most traditional husbands' comments indicated that they took the wife's career less seriously than did husbands in the professional group — less seriously in the sense of respecting it. Traditional husbands were less apt to talk of the wife having a contribution to make to her field or to society. They were more apt to see the wife's return to work as giving her something to do and people to talk to. It was therapeutic; it was like a hobby. For example, one man explained his views on the wife's future return to work as follows:

> I think of it . . . as something interesting so that she doesn't become the bored housewife that so many women become when the children grow up a bit. . . . [Her return to work] has been cast as an ancillary activity. . . . It's just giving her an outlet.

Others made comments like, "The arrangement we have is pretty suitable for us, where the wife's work is more of an avocation than a vocation." Or, "It wouldn't have to be a full-time job — just something to do and people to talk to. If she got away everybody would be better off. Anything — even volunteer work — would do it."

Secondly, most traditional husbands expressed some reservation about a career for the wife that would be involving in terms of time, emotion, and energy. They did not want it to detract from the family or from her role as wife and mother. One husband, who was very supportive of his wife's part-time work, expressed his strong disapproval of an involving career for her:

> *I don't think I would be very happy or could I really tolerate it if she felt that she had to work full-time and have a career in which she were very ambitious and had to tie herself into her career in which a great deal of work was demanded of her and feel that she was advancing through the ranks. . . . I don't think I could really tolerate that. . . . It would be impossible at that point to have a semblance of what I would consider a happy home life.*

Others mentioned things like the necessity of always recognizing the primacy of the needs of the children, or the fact that the wife could not have a career that would in any way upset the delicate balance of the husband's career.

Thirdly, traditional husbands were much less likely than husbands in professional couples to alter their own lives and provide concrete practical acts of support to make the second career in the family possible. Even two of the three traditional husbands with favorable attitudes toward a career for the wife did little to help make it a reality. This probably accounts for why these two traditional wives spontaneously reported conflicting expectations from the husband. One of these women first listed a number of reasons why her husband was in favor of a career for her, and then she told of his reasons against:

> *His reasons against — he has very high standards of homemaking. This attitude is pervasive about how hundreds of things are done. In putting it "for and against," he doesn't see it that way. He sees himself as for it. He sees the problems as practical difficulties that can be worked out. But I see them as obstacles — there are limits of time and energy.*

In this particular traditional couple, the husband expected high-quality homemaking even if she had a career, but was not willing to do any domestic tasks himself. Another wife commented about her husband saying, "He approves of my having a career, but he expects his house will run and his dinner will be ready and things like that." This was also a couple in which the husband did no domestic tasks.

Fourth, although traditional women talked about the husband's attitude, they did not stress its importance like the professional women did. The issue was not as salient for them. The professional women often brought up the issue spontaneously, often returned to it, and stressed it as essential. The traditional women did not see the husband's attitude as such a central issue in whether or not they combined career with marriage. There are at least two possible explanations for this difference. First of all, behavior that goes against the accepted norms is always more visible and more of an issue than behavior which follows the norms. Husbands in two-career families, by supporting and helping their wives, acted counter to prevailing norms; in contrast, traditional husbands followed prevailing norms. The second possible explanation involves the degree to which the woman's own motivation was an issue. In the traditional group there was no woman who was "determined" to have a career. They were either home-oriented or they were ambivalent, and among the latter none had resolved their own ambivalence to the point where the husband was the only factor preventing a career. In contrast, most of the professional women had solved any ambivalence to the point where they were committed to careers and serious about their work. For them an opposing husband would have been, in reality, a major obstacle to deal with. Some of the professional women actually either had refused to marry, or had divorced, men with unfavorable attitudes.

The interviews with the traditional group confirm the notion that for the two-career family to become an effective reality, both partners have to desire it and make this a basic assumption in their lives. Among the professional group, most couples took it as a basic assumption that the wife's career, as well as the husband's, was important. This pattern of expectations and assumptions was never found in the traditional group. The other three logical possibilities were found: couples where both partners assumed the woman should be primarily a wife and mother; couples where the wife was interested in a career, but the husband did not provide active support; and even one couple where the husband had helped his wife, but she preferred to be at home. There was, however, no traditional couple in which both partners took for granted the idea that it was important to have two careers.

NOTES

1. See respectively Erwin L. Linn, "Women Dentists: Career and Family," *Social Problems* 18 (Winter, 1971), p. 397; Margaret Hennig, "Career Development for Women Executives" (unpublished Doctor of Business Administration dissertation, Harvard University, 1970), pp. vii-10; Jane Gaudette Jones, "Career Patterns of Women Physicians" (unpublished Ph.D. dissertation, Brandeis University, 1971), p. 127; and, Jessie Bernard, *Academic Women* (New York: World Publishing Co., 1966), pp. 230-40. (First published 1964: Pennsylvania State University.)

2. Bernard, *op. cit.*, p. 231.

10

Breakdown: Divorce or Domesticity

> *I was no longer willing to pretend that I was inferior mentally, incapable of accomplishing anything.*
>
> Divorcee

> *Many reasons why women stay home involve the fact it is so complicated not to stay home.*
>
> Housewife

The fact that a family is a two-career family does not necessarily mean it will remain so. This type of life style can break down in at least three different ways. First of all, the marriage may end in divorce. Secondly, the wife may relinquish her career in favor of domesticity. Thirdly — a theoretical possibility but an empirical rarity — the husband may give up his career. The first two ways that the two-career family may break down are discussed here.

DIVORCE

The selection of a marital partner involves a certain risk. One can say that marriage is a mutual bet about life style. Both partners are gambling that the life style they envision for the future will be compatible with the life style the spouse wants to lead or will come to lead. They gamble that they will be compatible as to how they define their relationship, their family roles, their ambitions, each other's success, and many other aspects of the way they wish to live. And they may lose the bet. One spouse may fail to meet the other person's expectations. Or, over time, one spouse's expectations may change — but without the other person changing accordingly.[1] If the bet is lost, one way to solve the incompatibility is by divorce.

The Occurrence of Divorce Among the Women

Among all the professional and traditional women combined, there were six divorces which constituted a breakdown of a two-career family; that is, at the time of the divorce, the woman and her first husband each had a professional career.[2] The divorces of both professional and traditional women are discussed together, since there was no systematic difference between them. Among both groups of women the accounts of the process leading to the end of the marriage were quite similar. The only difference between the groups is that in the first instance of difficulty in combining career and marriage, two traditional women sacrificed the marriage, and the second time they sacrificed the career. The explanation for this seems to be in their attitude toward motherhood and mothering. These two women had neither wanted nor had children by their first husbands, but they did want and have children in the second marriage. For both of these women the greatest single obstacle to their pursuit of a career was their child-rearing responsibilities. They had difficulty getting help and they were worried about providing adequate mothering.

The independence of the women was a striking characteristic in the accounts all six gave of the divorce. They all described it either as being their own decision or as being a mutual decision between them and their first husband. As one explained:

> It was me that walked out. I said I'd had enough of this. This wasn't the way I was planning to live, and I just got up and went. . . . It was the smartest thing I've ever done.

Others made comments like, "I went off and got myself a divorce," or "We came to realize it was a mistake." These women never said it was primarily the husband who wanted the divorce, and they never talked about having been abandoned by the other partner. One wonders whether the accounts exaggerate the amount of independence of the women. Perhaps the person interviewed was unwilling to think of it, or report it, any other way. However, among the four men whose prior marriage ended in divorce, two of these said their wife had gone off with another man; so among the men, some did talk of having been left by the other partner.

The women described factors which, in their opinion, contributed to the divorce. They described ways in which they had lost the bet that their life style would be compatible with that of their first marital partner. The specific problems fell into two general categories: The first being differences as to how the partners defined the marital relationship, and the second, problems as to the relative emphasis placed on ambition vs. personal relationships. This is not to suggest that these factors were *the* cause of divorce. Rather, they were part of the whole complex of factors which led to the breakdown of the marriage.[3]

Definition of the Marital Relationship

One problem leading to divorce was a difference between partners in their definition of the marital relationship. Specifically, the partners differed in their ideas of how egalitarian the relationship should be. The wife thought it should have been more egalitarian than it was. As time went on, the wife was less and less willing to play the subordinate role. This manifested itself several different ways. In one couple it showed up in disputes over division of labor. Since the wife had a career, it was difficult for her to assume the domestic responsibilities without help. She did not think it fair that she should have to do all the domestic chores, and her husband do none. She explained:

> *One of the problems was that he wasn't very flexible in anything. I had to do everything. Well, I do a lot of work around here [in my present home]. . . . I don't mind doing work. But to be expected all the time to do all the work without any cooperation I think is not fair. . . . In my more mature attitude I look upon this as one of the things I felt was important in life — to have a partner that I could share some of the responsibility with.*

She went on to explain how helpful her present husband was. For example, he helped a great deal with the children and liked to do this. Something like that just would not have been possible with her former husband.

In two cases it was very important to the husband psychologically that he be superior to his wife. This became increasingly unacceptable to the wife, who preferred a more egalitarian marriage. In both these cases, the husband had strong feelings of competitiveness and a psychological need to "put down" the other partner. For example, one woman described how, when she and her first husband were both students, he could never resist showing how much cleverer he was by tearing her ideas to shreds. She elaborated as follows:

> *It was very destructive to me. He was a person who could never resist taking things apart. . . . Every single time I would think of something [for a master's thesis] I'd start to talk with him about it and in half an hour there wouldn't be anything left of it. And it wasn't just that. This was the way just about everything went, my opinions about anything. And you know, since we were both in the same field this was very painful. I don't think now that he was that much cleverer than I, (laughter) but it certainly seemed so at the time.*

This derision soon became intolerable. In the other case, the woman described a similar tendency to "put down" the wife. She said, "I'm afraid that because of his own psychological makeup, he more or less fostered this attitude that he was the great superior person, being awfully kind to pay any attention to me." Later, especially after she achieved greater professional success than her husband, this woman was no longer willing to play the subordinate role. She said, "I was no longer willing to pretend that I was inferior mentally, incapable of accomplishing anything, having to be supported and taken care of."

These cases support what was said in an earlier chapter about the current attitude which equates masculinity with superiority. Judging from the wives' interviews, both these husbands needed to constantly reassure themselves that they were indeed superior. The husband felt threatened by the wife even at a time when he — by objective criteria — was more successful. The first quote above is from a couple where the husband was always more successful than the wife. In the second case, the need to "put the wife down" had existed throughout all of the marriage, long before she began to achieve any professional success. She, however, eventually did outdo her husband. After several years of marriage, they went to graduate school together. He failed to get his degree. She had a baby and got her degree.

In another couple, there was a difference of opinion as to how much independence a wife should have. Specifically the woman complained that in her former marriage, her husband had not granted her enough independence. For example, if she had something important to do, such as some task at work, she was not free to just go ahead and do it. She practically had to ask his permission. She explained the difference between her marriages in this regard:

> *I'm my own boss — we cooperate and all that, but I have a reasonable amount of say as to what I'm going to do on a given day, which I didn't have before and that was a big factor. I think professional women like to have some feeling of independence. I don't mind being told what to do once in a while, but I like to know that if something is important enough I just go do it without asking a hundred questions.*

In each of the cases described, the two marital partners differed in their definition of what the marital relationship should have been. The wife objected to the inequalities between her role and the husband's role. The wife objected to the expectation that she be the submissive and subservient partner. She did not want to do all the housework. She did not want to be considered mentally inferior. She did not want to be denied independence.

Ambition vs. Personal Relationships

The other problems leading to divorce concerned how much emphasis should be placed on careerist ambitions vs. how much on personal relationships. In some respects this is related to the previous issue of differing definitions of marriage; after all, part of the definition of marriage is how important and salient the relationship is supposed to be. However, the present issue is broader. It also includes whether other personal and familial relationships, such as that between parent and child, should be important in a person's life. In these divorce cases, either one or both partners placed greater priority on career than on personal relationships. There might have been a difference of opinion, with one partner accusing the other of placing too much emphasis on career. Or, both partners valued their respective careers more than the marriage relationship.

These priorities manifested themselves several ways. For example, two women had complaints about the couple's allocation of time and effort. The issue was whether there would be any time for marriage and a home life, or was all time to be devoted to work. Each of these women said their husband was so wrapped up in his career that there was little time for her and for home. For example, in one couple where both spouses were students at the time, the wife explained:

> He spent a lot of time at school and it was a very competitive atmosphere [at his school]. I really got to know the inside of that department too. It was just dreadful. I finally decided one night as I was sitting home, because I was alone, . . . that you know, I might just as well be alone and be lonely, as be married and be lonely! (laughter)

In one of these couples, the woman saw how in the attempt to have two careers, not only did the husband "work too hard," but she did too. She explained:

> I was working very hard taking my exams . . . and my husband was working hard on his new job. We were all working too hard I guess and not relaxing enough. And that didn't contribute much to our mutual happiness. So after a while we just quit.

In this case, they both spent an enormous amount of time and energy on their careers; neither one had any time or leisure for the other. Maintaining a relationship under such circumstances was difficult.

These same two women also said that there was no room for children in their first marriage. As one said, "Career was very important . . . and children didn't figure into it." And the other explained, "He was so wrapped up in his own work that there wasn't much room for me in his life, and there wasn't any room for a family."

Decisions about geographic residence provide another example of how priorities were expressed. One divorced couple hardly ever lived together. After marriage, the spouses followed their own separate career interests and went different places. They married when both were graduate students. Right after the marriage, the wife left for Europe to do her graduate research. While she went to Europe, he stayed in the United States to work on his. Later he was in Europe for military duty, but by then she was teaching at a midwestern university in the United States. She said, "The following year, my husband was through with his service, and he got a job [an eastern university]. By then I realized we had been married several years but not living together." She got a job at another eastern university to be as close as she could to where he taught. But she soon decided they might as well "call it quits" and so she "went off and got herself a divorce." In this couple, the husband and the wife placed greater value on career ambitions than on the marriage relationship.

Thus, as these cases show, priorities were reflected in use of time and in decisions about where to live. It is difficult to maintain a relationship — except in name only — if one does not devote any time or attention to the relationship.

DOMESTICITY

Among the traditional couples, the two-career family structure broke down another way. Traditional wives sacrificed the career rather than the marriage when faced with problems of combining them. They did not rebel against playing the subordinate and supportive role in the marriage. They placed a higher value on fulfilling their family responsibilities than on furthering their own ambitions — on domesticity rather than on their own profession.

It is difficult to pinpoint *the* cause for a woman giving up her career. But, as the study has shown, if the wife is really serious about her career, then there will be a series of problems which the couple must somehow come to terms with to make two careers workable. Any one of these problems can be a reason for quitting one's profession. The most one can say is that in the account given by any one woman, some particular issue is especially salient. For example, one traditional woman stressed how she could never have a demanding job that might upset the delicate balance of her husband's career. One had her greatest difficulties in connection with trying to find help to babysit. Another was greatly hurt by her husband's move to another city. The list goes on and on; enough examples have been given throughout the study so that they need not be repeated here. The point is that a whole series of issues do exist, and any one can be dominant in a particular case.

The professional couples have shown that it is not impossible to surmount the difficulties involved in the two-career family. However, it must be emphasized that it may take a great deal of effort to do so. It should not be surprising if career motivation weakens in the face of such adversity. Many special arrangements have to be made if one wishes to go against the prevailing occupational and familial norms, and, as one traditional woman said, these arrangements are always in danger of breaking down. Just as one gets the arrangements made, something happens. She had been very career motivated at one time, but she had come to the conclusion that a career for a married woman involves "an extremely fragile arrangement which the slightest thing can knock over." Another woman spoke as follows about the complexities involved in working away from home:

Many reasons [why women stay home] involve the fact that it is so complicated not to stay home. . . . The problems of going back to work are such that it is much easier to stay home. . . . I cannot see leaving [the children] and getting so little out of it. I am frustrated but not unhappy.

She also had been quite career motivated at one time, and she "was very much torn" over the issue of whether to continue working. She had faced severe practical difficulties in hiring baby sitters and also emotional difficulties about leaving her children in the care of others. She finally decided that pursuing a career was not worth all the extra effort that was required to make it possible.

One would predict that more women would practice their professions if it were not so complicated for them to do so. Three of the seven traditional women curtailed their careers despite the fact that they had previously been very career motivated; and the other four, although their profession had never been a main priority, were interested in the work they had done. Professional life might have been more attractive to these women if it had not involved so many sacrifices and extra complexities. The surprising thing is not that some married women give up their careers. The surprising thing, given the present system, is that any two-career families exist at all.

NOTES

1. The idea of marriage as a mutual bet about life style is a generalization of an idea put forth long ago by Everett Hughes. Marriage, he said, is a mutual mobility bet. The partners are both betting that the other "can make it" as to social mobility. In the usual pattern, the wife is betting that the husband will "be successful." The husband is betting that the wife can be of help to him and can play the role of the wife of the kind of man he wants to become. Everett C. Hughes, private communication.

2. A total of seven women — four among the twenty professional women and three among the seven traditional women — were divorced. Six of these divorces are discussed here. One divorce is not analyzed here, since it was a traditional woman who did not even begin her attempt at a professional career until five years after her second marriage; thus this divorce did not constitute a breakdown of a two-career family. There were five previously married men. Of these, four were divorced. The other was a widower; however, the marital relationship had seriously deteriorated and the couple was living apart at the time of the wife's death. Only one of the five previously married men had originally had a wife with a career. In looking at the information on divorce, incidentally, it is important to remember that the study only picked up divorced people who subsequently remarried.

3. Goode, in his study of divorce, also analyzes many themes of complaint, without ever suggesting that they constitute *the* cause of the divorce. William J. Goode, *Women in Divorce* (New York: Free Press Paperback, 1965) pp. 113-32. (First published in 1956: Free Press.)

11

Toward Our Liberation

We have examined the life style of a group of two-career families and compared them with traditional families. We have seen how couples with two professions managed to carve out a life style for themselves. Looking at them and the obstacles they faced gives us clues as to how the larger society causes problems for the two-career family in general. It becomes clear that many of the problems they face are related to the inflexibility of occupations, the isolation of the small modern family, and the present definition of masculinity as superiority.

It is now time to think through the implications of the study. To begin with, some of the main findings that have been presented throughout the book will be briefly recapitulated. With these in mind, we will then examine the processes which perpetuate the status quo, discuss various value judgments that one might make about the existing system, and see what implications the findings have for changes which could be instituted that would help two-career families. This will lead us to some suggestions for change that should benefit both men and women.

RECAPITULATION

Professional and Traditional Couples Compared

We have seen throughout the book that the professional couples organized their lives in ways to combat many of the barriers to the two-career family. The degree to which they deviated from middle-class norms is apparent when their life style is contrasted to that of the traditional couples.

In deciding where to live, the career interests of professional wives were given much greater weight than were those of the traditional wives. The geographic residence of many men in the professional group was influenced by their wives' careers; among traditional men this hardly ever occurred. Most professional wives traveled alone on brief business trips, and in most cases the husbands were very supportive of their wives travelling alone. Since their marriage, the traditional wives had not travelled alone on business; they did not feel free to travel either because of the husband's attitude or because of practical difficulties in caring for the home in their absence. Most professional women de-emphasized the hostess role and gave only a minimum of professional parties associated with the husband's job. Traditional wives were more likely to elaborate the hostess role, and, in general, they saw this in positive terms.

Professional and traditional couples differed as to the division of labor within the home. Among professional couples the wives were not exclusively responsible for the performance of housekeeping or child-rearing tasks. Their burdens were lightened by employment of hired help and by assistance from the husband. Traditional couples retained a greater split between home as the wife's domain and career as the husband's domain. Regarding both housekeeping and child rearing, these wives were less likely to utilize hired help, and they received less assistance from their husbands. Over half these wives organized their lives completely around the aim of serving the husband and furthering his career. No professional woman completely arranged her life to serve her husband.

The groups also differed in how they matched the calendars of husband and wife — an issue of some importance since acceptance of career goals makes time a scarce commodity. In the professional group, the wife's own schedule was an important factor to be taken into account when matching calendars. In the traditional group, her schedule was considered unimportant and she adapted to the husband's routine.

In most professional couples the husband and wife said they did not experience a sense of competition with each other, despite the fact both had careers. In the traditional group spouses did not experience a sense of competition; but in a few cases where the wife valued a career, she made invidious comparisons because she had been relegated to the less prestigious role. In analyzing competitiveness between the sexes, the central issue does not seem to be segregated vs. non-segregated sex roles; rather, the central issue is that the culture equates masculinity with superiority.

The husband's attitude, as predicted, was an important factor in making two careers in one family possible. Almost all the men in the professional group had positive attitudes toward the wife having a career. They took the wife's work seriously in the sense of respecting it, and they translated their approval into concrete practical acts of support. In contrast, traditional husbands were less likely to have favorable attitudes toward a career for their wives. They took the wife's work less seriously, and they were less likely to alter their own lives and provide concrete practical acts of support to make the second career possible.

Men and Women Compared

The professional women can be compared either to other women or to men. Their relative career situation depends upon which of these comparisons one chooses to make. The discussion above, highlighting differences between professional and traditional couples, makes the former type of comparison. The major overall finding was that in many areas of life the career interests of the professional wives were given much greater weight than were those of the traditional wives. Thus, relative to other women they fare very well.

Relative to men — specifically their husbands — the professional women fare less well. Despite their great deviation from middle-class norms, most professional couples were still a great distance from equality of the sexes. Even though both careers were important, typically the man's career was still more important. For example, wives accommodated more to the husband's career needs than vice versa. If ambition and plans were altered, it was the wife who typically made the bigger sacrifice. If someone took a career risk when deciding where to live, it was the wife who made the gamble. Anti-nepotism rules, although technically applicable to either spouse, were always used against the women. If one partner was unaffiliated with an institution, or isolated from the mainstream of the profession, it was the woman. The woman's time — although valuable — was less valuable than the man's; for example, if one partner diverted time into hostessing professional parties, it was the woman who did so. And on the domestic side equality was also still lacking. No matter how much help the woman received, the domestic realm was defined ultimately as her responsibility; it was ultimately not defined as a responsibility to be shared equally by both spouses.

Thus, within the professional group, dilemmas resulting from two careers in one family were resolved more in favor of the husband than the wife. This outcome is in keeping with the current cultural expectation that this is the way it should be. In summary, two general conclusions can be drawn. On the one hand, the two-career couples deviated a great deal from middle-class norms. On the other hand, they were still a long way from equality of the sexes.

PERVASIVENESS OF MALE SUPREMACY

The fact that dilemmas in the two-career family were resolved more in favor of the husband means that we must look also at the issues of women's rights and male supremacy. Though there are a number of handicaps which women in this society now face in an attempt to have a career, all these really are sub-divisions of one major handicap: male supremacy. In other words, the main overall problem is that male supremacy has been, and to a large extent still is, seen as justified. Men are seen as more valuable than women. Although they pay a price for it in terms of pressures to succeed, men are selected to do the prestigeful activites in the society. Masculinity is equated with superiority, femininity with inferiority; and it has become part of the self image of *both* sexes to think in these terms.

The present study has focused on only one manifestation of male supremacy. It has looked at the dilemmas of having two careers in one family, and has shown the sex bias in how they are resolved. It has focused on problems which occur even when women get jobs despite discrimination, and even when women are highly motivated. For a complete understanding of the professional ramifications of male supremacy, one would also want to look at these other two aspects.

Outright discrimination in the professional world is also a manifestation of male supremacy, and it is a second way women are handicapped in their careers. Discrimination refers to things such as employers who, in their hiring, payment, promotion, and other policy decisions, take into consideration traits such as sex which are not directly relevant to the performance of the work. It refers to situations where employers systematically give jobs to men despite the presence of equally qualified female applicants, when graduate schools set low and arbitrary quotas on what percentage of an entering class can be female, when both sexes do the same work but the women have lower job titles or lower pay.[1] It is what Robert Townsend, that tongue-in-cheek critic of corporate organizations, means when he says "women are still bottom-of-the-heap." The giveaway is when you hear someone say, "Don't give her a raise; she's making a lot *for a woman.*"[2]

A third manifestation of male supremacy is the differential socializa- of the sexes. It too is a career handicap for women. Both in the family and in the school, women are trained in ways less conducive to careers than are men. Examples are the systematic training of women to be dependent, to be less achievement motivated than men, and to fear success. The opposite qualities are emphasized in the socialization of men.[3]

THE PERPETUATION OF MALE SUPREMACY

Since male supremacy is pervasive, it is important to look at the processes which perpetuate it. Occupations and the family, as they are now set up, form an alliance that tends to perpetuate male supremacy. In conjunction with each other, the rigid competitive work world and the isolation of the nuclear family support sexual inequality. Thus they make a self-perpetuating cycle. The three processes in this cycle are as follows. First of all, occupations and the family at present are structured in a way that promotes the career of the man. Secondly, in order to promote the career of the man, they hinder the career of the wife. Thirdly, since the wife does not have a career, she pours her energies overwhelmingly into child rearing, the result often being an emotionally overloaded mother-child relationship and thus a kind of interaction that can produce sons with narcissistic personalites who will seek self-aggrandizement through careers when they grow up. The details of these processes are discussed below.

Promoting the Man's Career

The family serves the occupational world by promoting the career of the husband in a number of ways. For one thing, the family, especially the wife, is expected to provide emotional support for the husband. The economy uses up men. High-level occupations are demanding of time and energy. The pressures of competitive effort and achievement create great tensions which the wife is supposed to offset by listening sympathetically and providing emotional support. For example, journalist William H. Whyte, Jr., in his studies of corporation life, writes about the wives of management and of how these women feel they must nurture the male ego. Describing their role as good listener, they speak of themselves as "sounding boards," "refueling stations," and "wailing walls." Whyte says management psychologists agree with the wives. He quotes one as saying that it is very important for a wife to let a man unburden the worries that he cannot admit to in the office.[4] Along a similar line, Slater writes of the "opiate role." Men, he says, are daily buffeted by the technological social structure they have created. And they tend "to use their wives as opiates to soften the impact of the forces they have set into motion against themselves."[5] Of course the wife's role may have a double-edged quality to it. While listening to the problems her husband has in the pursuit of success, she may also be pushing him to strive for success.

Further, the wife is expected to run the home in such a way as to facilitate the single-minded devotion of men to work. She is not to complain if his job comes first above all else. She is to run the home, rear the children, manage social obligations and do a multitude of other tasks so that the man does not have to use his valuable time to do them.

In addition, the family is expected to facilitate the mobility of men. If the man's job or career depends on moving, the family is expected to follow. The wife and children are not to have interests which would prohibit their moving to a new locale.

Hindering the Career of the Woman

The occupational and familial systems also perpetuate male supremacy by hindering the career of the woman in several ways.[6] First of all, if the wife does all she is supposed to do to help the husband, it is difficult to have a career of her own. Vice versa, if a wife has a career of her own, she cannot always be at the beck and call of her husband. In the present study, the professional and traditional women differed in how they resolved this issue. In the professional couples, no wife completely arranged her life just so as to serve the husband. In contrast, traditional couples tended to follow the norm. Over half the traditional couples had a very asymmetrical helping relationship. The wife organized her life so as to support and further her husband's career, but she did not receive comparable support from him. These traditional wives said things like, "When your husband comes home at 6:00 he needs you." "I haven't got a right to use that time which is really valuable to him." "It is the woman who serves the family."

The occupational world also hinders women by its rigidity. It gives preference to full-time and uninterrupted work. It gives preference to a person devoted to a careerist life style. It almost forces an "all or nothing" choice. Many women are unwilling to make the sacrifice required, even though they would work very well and effectively at a more flexible pace.

Further, the isolation of the nuclear family hinders the careers of women. The husband and wife are the only two adults around. The husband is expected to leave home each day to work. In the absence of other adult relatives, servants, or child-care centers, the wife is literally forced, in most cases, to remain home to care for the children when they are young. Arranging for child care was a major problem for both the professional and traditional women.

Sex Antagonism and Male Narcissism

The final link in the perpetuation of male supremacy is how women are influenced in the way they raise children by the present structure of occupations and of the family. Women end up being isolated at home because the competitive occupational world excludes them, and because our isolated families mean that there is seldom anyone except the mother available to care for the children. Thus the women become preoccupied with child rearing. The result is the over-loaded mother-child relationship and the maternal ambivalence which produce male children with narcissistic personalities. This male narcissism, in turn, keeps the cycle going.

Recent research suggests that these patterns of sex segregation and sex antagonism are part of a self-perpetuating cycle. Sex segregation continues: men predominate in high-level occupations, while women predominate in the family realm. Male supremacy continues: men are expected to do the more prestigious activities and women are relegated to the less prestigious line of achievement. This cycle of sex antagonism and male narcissism has been analyzed in a compelling way by Philip Slater. Discussing this syndrome as it occurred in both classical Greece and in modern middle-class America, the basic argument emerges that "a society which derogates women produces envious mothers who produce narcissistic males who are prone to derogate women."[7] The more the male imprisons the female in the home and absents himself from it, the more powerful the female is within the home and over her children.[8] This kind of segregation occurred in classical Greece. The Greek mother, Slater also observes, was very ambivalent toward her male child — alternately accepting him as an idealized hero and then rejecting his masculine pretensions. This type of maternal behavior, threatening to the son, produced males with a narcissistic personality structure. When adult, such males dealt with their fear of mature women by disparaging them — reassuring themselves that they had nothing to fear from so poor a creature. The disparaged women, in turn, raised another generation of narcissistic males. Thus the syndrome was perpetuated.

According to Slater, a similar cycle appears in modern middle-class American families. Again there is sex segregation, and there is maternal ambivalence. First, we see sex segregation in the pattern that has the father working away from home, limiting his participation in the family and leaving the mother dominant in child rearing. A male child, especially if he lives in an age-graded suburb, grows up in a female-dominated environment. Reality factors such as these constitute examples of sex segregation, no matter what people say they believe about the role of the sexes. Secondly, our era also has a set of factors which are especially conducive to maternal ambivalence; namely the underemployment of the educated female. Her knowledge and intelligence are under-utilized. Thus, she redirects her energies to child rearing:

> The middle-class female in modern America is expected to make a full-time activity out of a task — child rearing — which, throughout the history of mankind, has had to be worked into the interstices of a busy life. Whatever her talents, then, she tends to be hired as a kind of maternal Pygmalion — a molder of live persons. This is a task for which she may or may not be suited, but into which some frustration and resentment must inevitably creep, since she is unable, in such a setting, to realize her talents and is barred from the kinds of stimulation which her husband obtains through his work. As in the case of the Greeks, the male child is the logical vehicle for these frustrated aspirations, as well as the logical scapegoat for her resentment of the masculine monopoly in the major professions.[9]

The results are seen most clearly in education, with "the middle-class mother exhibiting a bizarre and fanatical obsession with the child's educational environment and achievements."[10] And, again, the result is to produce narcissistic males who will in turn derogate women.

Although gathering data on the relation between sex segregation and male narcissism was not the aim of the present study, some of the findings are relevant to the issue. They are in keeping with Slater's analysis. For example, only among the traditional group were there any cases of compensatory involvement with children. The professional women poured much of their energies directly into their own careers. In contrast, the traditional women expressed themselves vicariously through their husbands' careers or through their children. Two traditional women exhibited an extremely high degree of maternal possessiveness. In both cases it was with respect to a male child. This extreme possessiveness never occurred among the mothers who pursued careers of their own.

VALUES

We have reviewed what the research findings were in the study, and we have looked at the existing system and the factors which perpetuate it. A decision on what to do about these problems necessitates a thinking through of values.[11]

Alternative Models

There are various value positions one might adopt in response to existing sexual inequities. One might advocate elitism. Within the elitist framework, one might be either for male supremacy or for female supremacy. In contrast, more in keeping with American ideology, one might advocate egalitarianism. Within the egalitarian framework, there are also several sub-options. Three sub-options — the pluralist, the assimilation, and the hybrid models of equality — have been delineated by Alice Rossi.[12]

The pluralist model of equality refers to a society in which marked differences between groups — races, religions, sexes — are retained and valued for the diversity they create. Rossi states that in the case of sex, the pluralist model would invoke biological differences as necessitating the traditional sex role differentiation. This model sees woman's nurturance finding its best expression in maternity. Unfortunately, however, pluralism often disguises and rationalizes inequalities rather than really meaning that all groups have an equal footing of status, power, and rewards.

In the assimilation model of equality, the minority groups aspire to lose their distinctive characteristics and become absorbed into the mainstream of society. Regarding sex, an assimilation model would be the early feminist ideology: women are to seek equal places with men in the already existing prestigious positions of the society. The assimilation model does not advocate any change in the institutional structure of the society. It accepts the social institutions formed by the dominant group. But as Rossi notes, the traditional structure is precisely what many blacks, women, and members of the younger generation are now questioning and rejecting. Furthermore, the traditional structure depends on excluding women from top occupational positions.

In the hybrid model of equality there would be changes both in the dominant group and the minority groups. Using the medical profession as an example, Rossi explains the differences between the assimilation and hybrid models. Under the former, women should be motivated to seek medical careers like those pursued now by men. In contrast, "the hybrid model says . . . that the structure of medicine can be changed so that more women will be attracted to medical careers, and male physicians will be able to live more balanced, less difficult and [less] status-dominated lives."[13]

The hybrid model thus rejects the present institutional structure of society. Not only would the lives of women change; so would the lives of men. The hybrid model might require a greater change in the male than the female role since it would "involve a restructuring to bring the world of jobs and politics closer to the fulfillment of individual human needs for both creativity and fellowship."[14] Rossi elaborates:

> From this point of view, the values many young men and women sub-
> scribe to today are congenial to the hybrid model of equality: the desire
> for a more meaningful sense of community and a greater depth to per-
> sonal relations across class, sex and racial lines; a stress on human fellow-
> ship and individual scope for creativity rather than merely rationality
> and efficiency in our bureaucracies; heightened interest in the humani-
> ties and the social sciences from an articulated value base; and a social
> responsibility commitment to medicine and law rather than a thirst for
> status and high income.[15]

These all are examples of demands for change which have been made
by the younger generation, and, in our society, these demands "are
closer to the values and interests women have held than they are to the
values and interests of men."[16]

The Desirability of Hybrid Equality

The policy suggestions presented later are based on an assessment of
Rossi's hybrid model of equality as a desirable goal. It is important,
however, to emphasize that this is *not necessarily the value position
of the people who were interviewed for the study.* If the idea is brought
up for public discussion, more people may begin to see it as desirable.
The choice of this model here is based on practical, ideological, and
long-term preventive considerations. The hybrid model of sexual equality involves changing not only the woman's role, but also the man's;
it shifts the emphasis from the older issue of women's rights to the
newer issue of changing sex roles. On the basis of the practical, ideological, and preventive reasons discussed below, it seems desirable to
redefine the problem in this way.

The very practical reason for redefining the problem is that it will
never be possible to raise the status of women up to equality with
men if men's roles remain exactly as they are now. This is because
the current male role is predicated on the assumption that women are
to adapt their lives to the service of men. Thus only if *both* men's and
women's roles change will there be any possibility of equality of the
sexes. For example, as long as wives are expected to follow their husbands on an itinerant circuit of jobs, women will not become occupationally equal to men. As long as the husband's career predominates
over the wife's in determining where the couple will live, women cannot participate on an equal footing with men in the occupational world.
And as long as women have the major responsibility for the home,
they cannot participate on an equal footing with men in the occupational world. The present study has shown how both these issues —

where to live and division of labor in the home—typically are resolved in ways more favorable for the career of the husband than the career of the wife. Even the professional couples favored the husband's career more than the wife's — despite the fact that almost all these people thought it was important that the wife pursue her career. For example, even among the professional group, the careers of the wives, in general, were given less weight than the careers of the husbands when deciding on geographic residence. If someone took a risk when deciding where to live, it was the wife. If ambition and plans were altered, it was the wife who typically made the bigger sacrifice. And in the domestic realm, no matter how much help the woman received from her husband, it was still defined ultimately as her responsibility. Thus we see, from the study, that women cannot achieve equality with men under the current structuring of family and occupational life.

These results of the present study are substantiated by other analysts. Rossi states:

> No amount of entreaty will yield an equitable distribution of women and men in the top strata of business and professional occupations, for the simple reason that the life men have led in these strata has been possible only because their own wives were leading traditional lives as homemakers, doing double parent and household duty, and carrying the major burden of civic responsibilities. If it were not for the wives in the background, successful men in American society would have to be single or childless.[17]

A recent report of the Swedish Government to the United Nations is worth examining in this same connection. Most analyses and policy statements heretofore have stressed the idea of equality between men and women outside the home; they talk of equality in employment, voting, equal pay and the like. They have dealt less with the issue of equality within the home — that area which is both less prestigious and which, because of its private nature, is much more difficult to change by policy. But the Swedish report is a remarkable exception. As a government position paper, it is pioneering in the emphasis it gives to equality in the home and the emphasis it places on males increasing their participation in the domestic tasks of the home and the rearing of the children. It is worth quoting at some length:

> No decisive change in the distribution of functions and status as between the sexes can be achieved if the duties of the male in society are assumed *a priori* to be unaltered. . . . The division of functions as between the sexes must be changed in such a way that both the man and the woman in a family are afforded the same practical opportunities of participating in both active parenthood and gainful employment. If women are to

attain a position in society outside the home which corresponds to their proportional membership of the citizen body, it follows that men must assume a greater share of responsibility for the upbringing of children and the care of the home. . . . This aim can be realized only if the man is also educated and encouraged to take an active part in parenthood and is given the same rights and duties as the woman in his parental capacity. This will probably imply that the demands for performance at work on the man's part must be reduced: a continued shortening of working hours will therefore be of great importance.[18]

After discussing how women will not advance outside the home as long as men fail to assume their share of work within the home, the report goes on to talk of "male emancipation."

The expression "male emancipation" has therefore been coined in Sweden to denote the right of a husband to remain at home while the children are small where it is found more appropriate for the mother to devote herself to gainful employment. . . . In recent years demands have been made for a change in legislation whereby the father, like the mother (when she interrupts her career) would be entitled to a certain leave of absence with pay while the children are small.[19]

Linked to the discussion of "woman's role" in Sweden has been the notion that mothers *and* fathers of small children should have a choice between working inside or outside the home.

In addition to the practical reasons, there are ideological reasons for choosing the hybrid model of sexual equality as a desirable goal and for redefining the "woman problem" in terms of "changing sex roles." If one accepts as desirable the idea that a human being should be able to experience a wide range of feelings and activities in his or her lifetime, then both the present female and male role models leave a great deal to be desired. Both roles are limited. Women now are limited in that they are isolated from the mainstream of the society. They are deprived of meaningful activity which would give an overall direction and sense of purpose to their lives. Deprived of such activity, many engage in compensatory involvement with their children. There was a time in the past when the domestic female role was more meaningful. There was more to do around the home. Numerous people were in the home, and the woman was not isolated. Today, these conditions are changed. Housekeeping has been simplified. A woman, if at home, is isolated. Moreover, overpopulation has undercut the value of raising more children. Thus today, many women are without meaningful activities with which to occupy their time.

Men now are limited in that they are often estranged from familial relationships and non-work activities. Many men not only pursue careers, but "careerism." Achievement-motivated, competitive, and prestige-driven men often seek fame and success through single-minded devotion to work. Such pursuit of success is done at great emotional cost. First of all, only a very limited range of emotions and a limited part of the personality have a chance to be expressed. The more nurturant side of the personality that would be expressed in intimate friendship or familial relationships is subdued. Secondly, one never arrives at the plateau which can be called success: the goal merely recedes just as one approaches. Mobile big business leaders present extreme examples of the characteristics of "driven" men. One characteristic, as shown in the classic study by sociologists W. Lloyd Warner and James Abegglen, is their enormous concentration on their careers. They devote all their energies to it. This driving concentration is necessary for their advancement. But there is one great expensive flaw in the system — namely, there is no end to the cycle of departing and arriving and departing. "What is the point at which these men can stop, look back, and announce to themselves and their world that they have completed this long journey, that they will rest now? There does not seem to be such a point, for an essential part of the system is the need for constant demonstration of one's adequacy, for reiterated proof of one's independence."[20]

At least in the past, this narrow male role — and the emotional cost demanded by it — has fulfilled a need in the society: single-minded devotion to work helped to build the economy. The male work ethic poured a lot of energy into economic areas that otherwise would not have been so fully developed. However, not only does the narrow male role extract a great emotional price; one can also argue that it is no longer the kind of activity needed in the society. Men are still engaged in, and rewarded for, individual ambition. Service is not rewarded. Altruism is not rewarded. Yet it is these latter kinds of activities we need if we are going to solve the social problems of the nation. It is these latter kinds of activities we need if we are going to concern ourselves with the quality of life.

The current male ideal is not completely desirable as a goal. To suggest that women become equal to men who follow this kind of model would be merely to suggest that they switch from one type of deprivation to another. The professional couples are of interest in this regard. Most of the professional women fulfilled, or approximated, the "male" career model. In so doing, both husband and wife had meaningful activities, but it was at a certain price. This showed up most in their allocation of time and effort. Most professional women highly organized their use of time, and both husband and wife had hectic schedules. They made comments like "when the alarm goes off in the morning it's like the horses off at the races." "The routine is one that would discourage anyone." "In terms of time, our lives have been pretty much like a countdown for a rocket." Also, most professional women felt that they had given up activities or made sacrifices in order to pursue their careers. They were serious about their work and received gratification from it. But they recognized that they had given up things like social life, community involvement, and leisure reading in order to have the career. An even more extreme example comes from a recent study of female business executives. For the most part, these women followed a "male career model." They were very successful at it, but their success required certain sacrifices. Life outside of work was very restricted, especially during their first career decade. They greatly diminished their social life at this stage in order to devote more and more time to career. "During the twenty-five to thirty-five age period, there was minimal time devoted to rest, relaxation, and visiting family. Few maintained any sustained relationship with men outside work and most had only one or two close female friends (often sisters or other relatives)."[21]

Thus, both male and female roles are presently narrowly defined. To have women become like men would merely exchange one form of oppression for another. It would be a change from compulsive, competitive maternity to compulsive, competitive work. It would lead not to careers, but careerism.

A broader conception of sex roles, in which both men and women could partake of activities and emotions previously reserved for the other sex, would eliminate both these forms of deprivation. This newer view is often called an androgynous conception of sex roles. In one of her early statements on sex equality, Alice Rossi advocated a move in this direction. She stated:

> By sex equality I mean a socially androgynous conception of the roles of men and women, in which they are equal and similar in such spheres as intellectual, artistic, political and occupational interests and participation, complementary only in those spheres dictated by physiological differences between the sexes. . . . An androgynous conception of sex role means that each sex will cultivate some of the characteristics usually associated with the other in traditional sex role definitions.[22]

She elaborates, saying that tenderness and expressiveness would be approved of in men, while achievement need, workmanship and constructive aggression would be approved of in women. In addition to

Rossi's list of spheres where the sexes will be equal, the present analysis also advocates equality within the home.

The suggestion that women become more career-oriented is not new. The opposite suggestion, that men become less singlemindedly career oriented is a more recent idea. Even ten years ago, such a suggestion would have seemed absurd. But a lot has happened in the past decade to make it seem more feasible and desirable. Among the younger generation of college males, there is a trend away from the idea of leading status-dominated lives. There is a greater seeking of emotional relationships and of new career lines which will provide "more meaningful work." Describing the outlook of his generation, Mark Gerzon states the matter well: "The age of affluence and subsequent mass education have weakened the rationale for competitiveness and acquisitiveness for the members of this generation."[23] He notes that many highly qualified college graduates are turning away from business positions which previously, in terms of income and prestige, would have been considered prize finds. Among students today there is disaffection with business. "This generation is concerned about the openness and fullness of interpersonal relations. A business occupation seems to be far from ideal for young people searching for such a way of life."[24] It is from this point of view that Gerzon explains the overwhelming box-office success of the movie, *The Graduate*. The hero could have "made it big" — with the big house and the big name. But he did not want to. He refused to accept the emotional emptiness that he saw beneath the affluence and propriety of "successful society." The movie appealed because "it told the story of a young man growing up in a society he could not accept, the same story that millions of young moviegoers knew so well."[25]

This desire — even among men — to escape status-dominated lives is seen in the employment trend among many young professionals. Many no longer wish to follow the routes defined as prestigious a decade ago. One example is the shift in employment trends of top law graduates. A 1958 *Harvard Law Review* issue reports that twenty-six out of twenty-eight law review editors who had taken jobs were going to clerk for judges or work for large law firms. Twelve editors were going to the larger "Wall Street" firms, and eight were going to large firms in other cities.[26] Now, however, the movement is away from big-name firms and toward public service or activist jobs. Of the 39 *Harvard Law Review* editors who graduated in June 1970, not one intended to join a high-paying Wall Street law firm. Instead, most planned to enter neighborhood agencies or government service — and represent the individaul against the institutions.[27]

The empty promise of the narcissistic male role has also been discussed recently by Slater. He talks of "career" as a stern Calvinistic word. It connotes a rigorous life pattern to which everything pleasurable, human, and emotional is ruthlessly subordinated. When a man asks a woman if she wants a "career" in this sense, it intimidates her. Slater suggests that a more effective response would be for her to reply that a "career" thus defined is a pernicious activity for *any* person to be engaged in; it should be eschewed by both men and women. Of course she does not want this kind of "career"; she wants some kind of meaningful and stimulating activity. Slater suggests that women should not accept the definition of inferiority which is imposed upon them because they do not pursue work with Calvinistic fanaticism. Rather, they should make a more revolutionary response. They should argue that woman's unwillingness to sacrifice a host of human values to personal narcissism and self-aggrandizement through careerism makes her the superior sex.

> Such a stance would in fact liberate both sexes: women would be freed from the suffocating stagnation of the artificial domestic role in which they have been imprisoned; men would be liberated from their enslavement to the empty promise (ever receding, always redefined as just out of reach, and unsatisfying even when grasped) of "success."[28]

In addition to the practical and ideological reasons, there is a third reason — a preventive one — for accepting the hybrid model of sexual equality as a desirable goal. Whereas previously we were talking of remedial measures for redressing sexual inequalities, here we are talking of ways to prevent the inequalities from arising in the first place. We have reviewed recent research which suggests that the patterns of sex segregation and sex antagonism are part of a self-perpetuating cycle. If one accepts this analysis, then a logical suggestion to break this cycle is to change the adult roles of *both* sexes.

One change needed is to make women less envious of male prerogatives and thus less likely to engage in compensatory involvement with their children. This can be done by increasing women's participation in careers — a goal which is desirable in its own right as previously discussed. But this change alone is not enough. It would still leave children, including male children, to be reared almost exclusively by women. And as long as the male child's world is dominated by females, then as an adult he will have to prove his superiority to adult women to prove he is not a child. Thus to break the cycle, one must also change the role of adult men and increase their participation in the rearing of children.

SUGGESTIONS FOR CHANGE

Most of the barriers to achieving a hybrid model of sexual equality and to sustaining the two-career family are associated with two major factors: the rigidity of occupations and the isolation of the nuclear family. Thus, if one wants to promote sexual equality and reinforce the two-career family, one should remove these obstacles.

Changing the Occupational World

To encourage the two-career family, occupations should be made less rigid. One of the more important and obvious ways to do this is to promote flexible work schedules — for women *and* men. There are two issues here — which hours to work and how many hours to work.

A flexible schedule means having some choice over which particular hours one will work, even though the total number of hours may remain constant. As the present study showed, the women who combined career with major responsibilities for child rearing often found flexibility of hours more important than the absolute number of hours involved. When working hours of their own choosing, it was easier to manage their private lives. For example, it might be easier to work every morning and every evening, rather than eight to five, because the former made it possible to spend time with children after school. Or perhaps it was easier to work nine to six rather than eight to five, because that made it easier to get the children off to school. To the extent that men increase their participation in child rearing, flexibility of hours will be increasingly important to men as well as women.

Flexibility of work schedules also involves the idea that a person, especially when his or her children are young, should be able to work "less than full time." This need not necessarily mean half time. In the present study, those women who by choice worked less than full time often found it possible to work at a rate of ⅔, ¾, or ⅞ of what men did. In other words, they merely made a slight reduction in their work load in order to accommodate both career and family. To the extent that men increase their participation in child rearing, this option will be increasingly important to men as well as women.

This option of flexible work should not involve undue penalties. For example, the prevailing practice of severely penalizing part-time people should be abandoned. One should be able to work less than full time without becoming a second-class citizen — without losing employees' fringe benefits, without losing professional status, or, if a student, without being denied scholarships.

At first glance, it might seem that flexible hours and less than full-time work would be too much of a hardship from the employer's or the school's point of view. But in actuality, these suggestions are merely an *extension of existing practice*. It is important to stress that administrative machinery *already* exists to program work in a great variety of flexible ways. Employers and schools already make many special arrangements regarding flexible work, but they do it only for "socially acceptable reasons." It is often possible to work at a given place part time — if one is combining this with paid employment elsewhere; for example, teaching part time one place and doing research elsewhere. Or it is possible to work part time if one simultaneously returns to school. These are acceptable reasons. Flexible schedules are common in other situations too — in cases where it is clearly to the employer's advantage. This is done when employers need additional people for rush hour or for the busy season of the year. And it is done when certain categories of labor are scarce; for example, when secretaries or nurses are in short supply, employers are more willing to accept their requests for flexible hours of their own choice. The point is that, in many cases, flexible schedules are already an accepted practice. The suggestion to do this for men or women with small children is thus merely an extension of existing practices. What needs to be done is to define familial responsibilities as a valid and "socially acceptable" reason for obtaining flexible work schedules.

The Women's Caucus at the 1969 meeting of the American Sociological Association put the matter well. The resolutions it presented to the business meeting included the following statement:

> Twenty-six per cent of the full-time male faculty in graduate departments today are joint appointments at a senior rank. If a department can thus share a man with another department, it can as readily share a man or a woman faculty member with a family.[29]

As the caucus clearly saw, joint appointments between two departments are already common practice. All that is needed is to extend the practice — to have, so to speak, "joint appointments between work and family."

Changing schedules is only one of the more obvious ways to increase the flexibility of work. Many other occupational assumptions also might be challenged. Practices are often retained in an unthinking way, without evaluating whether the work might not be done just as well, or even better, some other way. The hostess role is a good example. One might ask whether the wife's participation as hostess really is so necessary. Why not eliminate the more tedious of the quasi-business, quasi-social gatherings altogether? The experience of the couples interviewed suggests that there is a great deal of lattitude in the amount of entertaining one really "must" do. For example, most of the professional women deemphasized the hostess role. They gave only a minimum of professional parties associated with the husband's job, and yet their husbands were very successful. As for those business socials deemed absolutely necessary, these events could be run by a person — either male or female — who is paid to do this. Just as one hires social secretaries, the role of host or hostess could be a paid occupation in and of itself. Epstein has raised a similar issue when speaking of the First Lady. She notes how the President's wife is required to give constant attention to the protocol side of affairs of state. She considers this an example of the large-scale exploitation of women at the sides of their husbands. If the President's wife is required to do all this work, she might at least get paid for it.[30]

There are many other ways in which occupations could be made more flexible and many other assumptions that might be questioned. Fortunately, there seems to be a trend toward thinking in these terms. Addressing the problems of women in careers, many writers have come up with suggestions that would increase the flexibility of occupations, and very often their suggestions would apply to men as well as women. For example, Alice Rossi presents a very critical analysis of the criteria now used to evaluate academic productivity. At present the main focus is on things such as number of publications, number of professional organization memberships, number of offices held in professional organizations. She suggests that a larger range of things — quality of teaching, service to the institution and community, etc. — be included in the criteria on which an academic man or woman is evaluated. "No one has conducted research on academic productivity with this enlarged net of criteria, and it is a moot point whether men would show greater productivity than women if such criteria were applied."[31]

Writing on women in the academic world, historian Patricia Graham suggests ways that the tenure regulations could be made more flexible. She notes that the time when a person normally is trying to attain tenure coincides with a woman's childbearing years. Thus the greatest pressures for scholarly publication and for domestic performance often occur at the same point in a person's life. "One way of handling this difficulty is to grant women assistant professors [the option of] an automatic 1-year extension, before the tenure decision is made, for each pregnancy they have, up to a maximum of two, during their nontenure years."[32] Other analysts have focused on the idea of redefining maternity leave. Several, wary of granting privileges solely to women and not men, have suggested that "parenthood leave" be granted to *both* men and women — on the grounds that the birth and care of a new child is a *family* event in which both parents might wish to participate. In addition, others have taken a new look at anti-nepotism rules and now are questioning the validity and constitutionality of these rules.[33]

Thus many analysts starting with the problems of women's careers, have come up with a variety of suggestions about how to make the occupational world more flexible for women and men. The specific examples mentioned here deal with academia. But people in other lines of endeavor probably can think of similar ways to change their work settings. Certainly the problems encountered are common to many professions. As women strive to establish themselves on career ladders — whether in medicine or business or whatever — they are also expected to found and care for families. What is needed are new definitions of work and career lines — things such as the innovative residency program in psychiatry developed at New York Medical College. Known as the "mother's program" in psychiatry, it was designed to provide flexible training by such things as enabling a resident to work nine months out of each year and thus be free during the children's vacations. What is needed are more such imaginative programs.

Changing the Family

If one wants to promote women's careers and sexual equality, policy should also be directed at the isolated nuclear family. Most importantly, changes should be made to alleviate the enormous difficulties which the isolation of the small modern family creates for child rearing and for the socialization process.

Here also changes should be made for both immediate practical reasons and long-term preventive reasons. The present isolation of the small family means that there is seldom anyone around to help the wife with her tasks. This leaves the woman primarily responsible for housekeeping and child rearing. This pattern was seen to have several drawbacks. On the practical level, it means that those women who do have careers often have "two jobs" — work and home. As to long-term effects, it means that women who do not work often have so little to do that is meaningful that they engage in compensatory involvement with their children; these women — through an over-loaded mother-child relationship — perpetuate the cycle of sex segregation and male narcissism. Thus for both immediate pragmatic and for long-term preventive reasons, the woman's isolation in, and *de facto* domination of, the home should be changed. This can be done by increasing the father's role in child rearing, and by providing child-care centers — with both male and female staff.

The father's participation in child rearing would be facilitated by a change already discussed — namely, by promoting more flexible work schedules for men as well as for women. The present study has shown, for example, that only couples with flexible schedules had the option open to them of sharing child care during the day. Several husbands in the professional group had done a lot of day-time baby sitting, and for a few couples the solution for many years was for the husband and wife to take turns being at home to look after the children.

Establishment of day-time child-care centers is a particularly crucial change that would encourage the two-career family and promote equality of the sexes. As shown by the couples studied, it is difficult for a parent in a two-career family to combine professional and child-rearing responsibilities because there are no *collective* solutions to the problems it raises. Only individual solutions currently exist. At present each two-career couple has to make their own individual arrangements for child care. This usually means employing help within one's own private home. This solution is both expensive and inconvenient. Even if a couple can afford help, it may become a major and time-consuming problem merely to find someone to employ. Group care for children would remove a major barrier to a mother's participation in activities outside of the home.[34]

Most of the professional women interviewed expressed positive attitudes about day-time child-care centers. Specifically, two thirds of these wives had favorable views. In perhaps the most strongly worded reply, one woman spoke as follows:

> *I think this is one of the shames of the United States that this does not exist and I think that any effort that could be made for the proper daytime care for children of working mothers deserves an enormous amount of public investment. I think it's disgraceful that it hasn't been done. . . . I think it would be a solution to a social problem which is full of indignity. . . . I myself went to kindergarten and nursery school very happily. I have very positive feelings about group care of children and group activity.*

Those women favoring day-care centers saw them as desirable for a variety of reasons. This method of child care would be less expensive than hired help in private homes. It would be easier to get trained people to work in centers. Individual families would be saved the labor of having to make their own arrangements. Many of these women qualified their answers by saying that day-care centers would be good if they were in convenient locations, if they were used in moderation (e.g., part time), and if the center "was a good one." A few women gave mixed replies. They preferred to have their children cared for within the private home, but they thought it would be good to have such centers available — either for times when one could not get qualified help to work within the home or for other mothers who would want to use them. Only one of the twenty professional wives had strong negative feelings about such centers. She felt that "shuffling your children off somewhere" would indicate you did not want them, and believed that "it hurts your mother instinct a little bit." Yet this woman, did send her children to nursery school and had positive views about doing so. In fact, all four mothers who expressed either mixed or negative views about child-care centers sent their children to nursery school. Of these four, three were enthusiastic about nursery school — a fact which suggests that they were reacting more against a stereotyped image of the term "child-care center" rather than being against group care of children *per se*.

Most of the husbands in the professional group also had positive attitudes toward day-time child-care centers. Several qualified their answers by saying that such centers would be good if they were used part time and if they were a complement, rather than a replacement, to the care given by the parents. Only a few husbands expressed negative attitudes; they thought "farming-out" of children was wrong or they thought the child had more freedom in his own home.

For people at the socio-economic level of the couples interviewed, private or cooperative nursery schools provide the services which, in other countries, one can obtain through public child-care centers. Almost all the professional couples with children had sent them to nursery school. This is an option that was available to them because of their relatively high income level, and it is, of course, a private solution to a public problem.

The United States is notoriously lacking in child-care centers, especially nonprofit facilities. Thus, even when the services are available, they are still typically considered a privilege which one must purchase individually, rather than a right which is to be paid for by the community. The figures are given below. A 1968 report states:

> The number of children being cared for in licensed day care facilities has increased from fewer than 200,000 in 1963 to more than 500,000 in 1968, but the facilities do not begin to meet the need of many millions of children under 14 years of age whose mothers now work and who need supervised care during all or part of the working day, either in pre-school day care facilities or after-school centers.[35]

Alice Lake discusses both the capacity of existing day-care centers and the type of ownership. In 1970, she observed, licensed centers were caring for about 500,000 children, less than 12 percent of the need.

Though a handful of these have been run by government, churches, or charitable groups, in 1970 almost 60 percent were commercial operations, small businesses run for profit.[36] Thus, in a large percentage of these centers, the parents are customers who pay to leave their children.[37]

Though the past two years have seen the growth of the day care movement in the United States, a great deal remains to be done. The United States should follow the lead of such countries as Sweden, Denmark, and the Soviet Union in actively promoting child-care programs. These child-care centers should be seen as a positive good. They should be established with the idea that they will not only free women, but that they will constitute a positive and valuable experience in the child's development. For a long time in the United States, both public opinion and academic analysts emphasized the dangers of maternal deprivation.[38] And a mother's employment was defined as maternal deprivation whether it led to the child being cared for by a mother substitute either individually or in a group. From this older point of view, child-care centers at best seemed an unfortunate necessity — a regrettable form of child care inferior to continual attention from the mother. More recently, however, people have begun to emphasize the opposite peril; namely, the dangers of the mother-child relationship in which the mother's main preoccupation is giving continual care to her children.[39] From this more recent perspective, child care centers can be seen as more desirable. They are one way of diluting the emotional overload of the mother-child relationship. Both mother and child would benefit.[40]

A major portion of the expense of establishing and operating such centers could be paid for by public government funds. The United States, up to now, has privatized child rearing far more than many other countries. Using public funds for day-care would be one step toward redefining child rearing as a responsibility of the society, not just the individual.

Pushing for government support of child-care centers should not preclude urging other organizations, such as schools and employers, to also establish and support centers. Businesses, hospitals, industrial plants, and universities are obvious examples of organizations that should be prodded into founding and subsidizing child-care centers. Students should urge that schools and universities provide day-care. Not too long ago, schools and universities were faced with the necessity of adapting to married students; they did so by providing married-students' housing, revising the stipulations of scholarships, and making other changes. Now they must go one step further and adapt to students who are parents. Employees should argue for day-care as a fringe benefit of employment. It has become standard practice in many places for an employee to have things such as life insurance and medical insurance subsidized by the employer. Now this idea should be extended to include subsidizing day-care.[41]

Day-care centers will not be acceptable to parents unless certain standards are met. For example, many of the women interviewed who were in favor of centers, qualified their answers. They said the center should "be a good one," be used "in moderation" (e.g., part time), and be in a "convenient location." The qualifications they made are useful in thinking about what the centers should be like.

First of all, the day-care center should have safe physical facilities and have competent personnel. The women's definition of "a good center" included both these aspects. One woman, referring to a combination nursery school and supervised play program her daughter had attended, elaborated as follows:

There are several fairly minimal things. . . . They should not be crowded. There shouldn't be too many children per supervisor. They should be clean and spacious and have equipment and all the usual things. But in addition I suppose mainly it's my own sense of the personality of the people involved. And the lady who teaches there . . . is someone I admire very much. . . . She has an excellent relationship with the children. She's firm without being tyrannical, and takes a great deal of individual interest in them, draws them out.

Thus the physical quality of the setting and the skill of the personnel are both crucial.

Secondly, the centers should have options as to the amount of time a child can attend, and they should be noncompulsory. Parents could thus decide for themselves what proportion of time would be appropriate for their child to spend at the center, and those parents who object to such care would not have to use the centers at all.

Thirdly, day-care centers should be in convenient locations. Establishing them at places where the parents work would seem to be optimal from several points of view — the child's, the parent's, and the administrator's. Locating centers at work would make it easy for parents to stop by during the day. The parents could see their children at coffeebreak or over the lunch hour, take them for a walk, and meet the children's friends. The children would thus be drawn more into the community, rather than being left in some isolated far-distant place. Locating centers at the place of employment would also eliminate the need for any additional travel on the part of the parent to take the child to the center — an issue of some importance given that time is at a premium. Locating day-care centers at work also makes sense administratively. A group of people needing the center is already gathered in one place. A university is an obvious example; students, staff, and faculty members needing the day-care facilities are already gathered together in one place.

Two other suggestions, although not mentioned in the interviews, deserve special discussion: the sex composition of the staff and the idea of community control. Suggestions for the sex composition of the staff are based on the findings of other researchers. And community control is an issue that has been receiving more and more attention since the study was carried out.

The staff of a day-care center should include males as well as females. This should be done on much more than a token basis. It may not be possible to have a 50-50 ratio immediately, but recruitment, hiring, and employment policies should have this as an aim. Moreover, this 50-50 ratio should hold at all ranks of employment. One would not want all the supervisory positions to go to men and lower positions to women. There are three reasons for employing both sexes. First, it is in keeping with the idea that equality of sexes means that jobs and occupations are not to be sex linked. Secondly, it would be one way of changing the image of child rearing from an all-female task to one done by both males and females. Females predominate now in child rearing in the home, in nursery schools, and in elementary schools. Although individual men often enjoy working with children, public opinion tends to ridicule them for it. Thirdly, and very importantly, it would change the developmental experience of the child. This would be one way of helping to break the cycle described previously which perpetuates male supremacy; that is, as long as male children are raised by females, then as adults they have to prove they are superior to adult women. Having experience as a child with authorities of both sexes would eliminate the association in men's minds between female authority and childhood.

The last suggestion is that child-care centers be subject to community control; that is, that members of the group served have an active voice in the policy-making decisions of the center. Community control is an issue that has come up increasingly for discussion in the last two years. While the push for day-care has gained momentum, the spectre looms large of a government bureaucracy rearing children in an impersonal way or big business sacrificing children for its own profits. One should not overlook these dangers, for they are very real. For example, Alice Lake's recent article talks of the inadequacies of many of the commercially run centers: too often, there is a constant battle between the owner's financial balance sheet and the child's needs.[42] With the growth of day-care centers well under way, the question now is perhaps not whether the trend will grow, but in what direction. Community control is one way of making sure that the growth is in a beneficial rather than detrimental direction.

SUMMARY

Thus we have seen that most of the barriers facing the two-career family are related to two major factors — the rigidity of occupations and the isolation of the nuclear family. And these in turn are related to the vicious cycle of male supremacy. Changes which would help bring about equality of the sexes by attacking these problems include promoting flexible work schedules for women and for men, increasing the father's role in child rearing, and establishing child-care centers. As the present study showed, having two careers in the same family is particularly difficult now because each couple must invent their own *ad hoc* solutions to the problems it raises. The changes proposed are an attempt to replace these strictly individual solutions with collective ones and institutionalized ones.

The present study dealt specifically with couples in which the wife had a professional career, but certainly the changes recommended above would benefit working women in general, irrespective of what type of job they had, and would also benefit many men. They would benefit any person seeking to avoid confinement in the narrow male and female roles presently prescribed in our society.

NOTES

1. For some examples of current discriminatory practices in education and employment see the symposium on women and the law, *Valparaiso University Law Review*, 5 (Symposium Issue, 1971), pp. 203-488; and Caroline Bird, *Born Female: The High Cost of Keeping Women Down* (New York: David McKay, 1968).

2. Robert Townsend, *Up The Organization* (Greenwich, Conn.: Fawcett Publications, 1971), p. 145. (First published in 1970: Alfred A. Knopf.) (Emphasis in the original.)

3. Relevant discussions of the differential socialization of the sexes include: Mirra Komarovsky, "Functional Analysis of Sex Roles," *American Sociological Review*, 15 (August, 1950), pp. 508-16; Matina S. Horner, "Woman's Will to Fail," *Psychology Today* (November, 1969), pp. 36-38 and 62; and Alice S. Rossi, "Equality Between the Sexes: An Immodest Proposal," *Daedalus*, 93 (Spring, 1964), pp. 638-46.

4. William H. Whyte, Jr., "The Wives of Management," *Man, Work, and Society*, eds. Sigmund Nosow and William H. Form (New York: Basic Books, 1962), pp. 548-55. (First published in 1951: *Fortune*.)

5. Philip E. Slater, *The Pursuit of Loneliness: American Culture at the Breaking Point* (Boston: Beacon Press, 1970), p. 74.

6. Someone who sees very clearly that to preserve the status quo one would have to continue to deny equal occupational opportunity to women is Parsons. In context, it is clear that his own preference is to preserve the existing system. See, for example, Talcott Parsons, "The Social Structure of the Family," *The Family: Its Function and Destiny*, ed. Ruth Nanda Anshen (New York: Harper, 1949), p. 196.

7. Philip E. Slater, *The Glory of Hera: Greek Mythology and the Greek Family* (Boston: Beacon Press, 1968), p. 45.

8. *Ibid.*, p. 8.

9. *Ibid.*, pp. 450-51.

10. *Ibid.*, p. 451.

11. A detailed analysis of value-laden assumptions (e.g., being pro change or pro status quo) and how they influence research and the conclusions drawn from research has been done in a separate paper. Lynda Lytle Holmstrom, "Talcott Parsons and the Feminine Mystique: Assumptions Underlying Research," (unpublished manuscript, Brandeis University, 1968).

12. Alice S. Rossi, "Sex Equality: The Beginnings of Ideology," *The Humanist* (Sept.-Oct., 1969), pp. 3-6 and 16.

13. *Ibid.*, p. 16.

14. *Ibid.*

15. *Ibid.*

16. *Ibid.*

17. *Ibid.*, p. 6.

18. Maj-Britt Sandlund, *The Status of Women in Sweden: Report to the United Nations, 1968* (Stockholm: The Swedish Institute, 1968), p. 4.

19. *Ibid.*, p. 6.

20. W. Lloyd Warner and James C. Abegglen, *Big Business Leaders in America* (New York: Harper, 1955), p. 83.

21. Margaret Hennig, "Career Development For Women Executives" (unpublished Doctor of Business Administration dissertation, Harvard University, 1970), p. vi-15. Also of interest is the discussion of the "Overload" dilemma facing dual-career families in Michael P. Fogarty, Rhona Rapoport, and Robert N. Rapoport, *Sex, Career and Family* (London: George Allen and Unwin Ltd., 1971), pp. 341-44.

22. Rossi, "Equality Between the Sexes: An Immodest Proposal," p. 608.

23. Mark Gerzon, The Whole World Is Watching: A Young Man Looks At Youth's Dissent (New York: Viking Press, 1969), p. 92.

24. Ibid., p. 95.

25. Ibid., p. 134.

26. Anon., "Editors' Employment," Harvard Law Review, 71 (March, 1958), pp. vii-viii, cited in Erwin O. Smigel, The Wall Street Lawyer (New York: Free Press, 1964), p. 39.

27. Anon., "The U.S.'s Toughest Customer [Nader and his Raiders]," Time (December 12, 1969), p. 98.

28. Slater, Pursuit of Loneliness, p. 73.

29. Peter H. Rossi, "Minutes of the First Business Meeting September 3, 1969," The American Sociologist, 5 (February, 1970), p. 64.

30. Cynthia Fuchs Epstein, Woman's Place: Options and Limits in Professional Careers (Berkeley: University of California Press, 1970), p. 114.

31. Rossi, "Sex Equality," p. 16.

32. Patricia Albjerg Graham, "Women in Academe," Science, 169 (Sept. 25, 1970), p. 1289. Harris reports that a "concession has recently been made by Princeton, where nontenured women faculty may, at their option, delay their tenure decision if they find that family responsibilities make it difficult for them to complete the necessary publications within the normal seven-year limit." Although Harris herself sees child-care facilities as the better solution, she nevertheless characterizes the change in tenure regulations as helpful. Ann Sutherland Harris, "The Second Sex in Academe," AAUP Bulletin, 56 (Sept., 1970), p. 294.

33. Pauli Murray, "Economic and Educational Inequality Based on Sex: An Overview," Valparaiso University Law Review, 5 (Symposium Issue, 1971), p. 265; and Anon., "Faculty Appointment and Family Relationship," AAUP Bulletin, 57 (June, 1971), p. 221.

34. Other studies of problems facing women have also suggested child-care centers. See, for example, Anon., Special Report On Women and Graduate Study ("National Institutes of Health: Resources For Medical Research, Report No. 13"; Washington, D.C.: U.S. Government Printing Office, 1968), p. vii and p. 34; and Jane Gaudette Jones, "Career Patterns of Women Physicians" (unpublished Ph.D. dissertation, Brandeis University, 1971), pp. 144-45.

35. The Interdepartmental Committee On the Status of Women, American Women: 1963-1968 (Washington, D.C.; U.S. Government Printing Office, 1968), p. 6.

36. Alice Lake, "The Day-Care Business: 'Which comes first — the child or the dollar?' " McCall's (November, 1970), p. 96. A recent newspaper article gives somewhat different figures stating that 640,000 licensed day-care spaces are available and more than one third are privately run. Nancy Hicks, "Day Care: Demand Outrunning Growth," New York Times, Nov. 30, 1970, p. 1. More detailed analyses of day care are just beginning to be published. Roby, in a forthcoming book, deals with the need for day care, examines past United States' experience with child care as well as the policies

of other nations, and makes suggestions for what we might do in the future. Pamela Roby (ed.), *Child Care — Who Cares?: Foreign and Domestic Infant and Early Childhood Development Policies* (New York: Basic Books — in press).

37. The issue of profit vs. nonprofit centers is mentioned here because it raises the question of whether day-care is to be a privilege or a right. This is somewhat different from another issue that gets discussed whenever one mentions "the day-care business"; namely, can a profit-oriented organization ever do a high-quality job of child care. However, there seems to be no *a priori* reason to assume that a profit-oriented center necessarily would do a bad job and a government (or other non-profit) center would do a good job; likewise, there is no *a priori* reason to assume the opposite either.

38. For a review of literature on maternal deprivation, from opposing points of view, see Joseph B. Perry, Jr., "The Mother Substitutes of Employed Mothers: An Exploratory Inquiry," *Marriage and Family Living* 23 (Nov. 1961), p. 362.

39. See, for example, Arnold W. Green, "The Middle-Class Male Child and Neurosis," *American Sociological Review*, 11 (February, 1946), pp. 31-41; A. C. Spectorsky, *The Exurbanites* (New York: J. B. Lippincott, 1955); Kenneth Keniston, *The Uncommitted: Alienated Youth in American Society* (New York: Harcourt, Brace, and World, 1955); Rossi, "Equality Between the Sexes: An Immodest Proposal"; Warren G. Bennis and Philip E. Slater, *The Temporary Society* (New York: Harper and Row, 1968), p. 91; and Slater, *The Glory of Hera.*

40. Opinion in certain other countries, such as the U.S.S.R., goes even one step further in justifying *group* care of children; positive good is seen as resulting from the collective experience *per se*. See David R. Mace, "The Employed Mother in the U.S.S.R.," *Marriage and Family Living* 23 (Nov., 1961), pp. 330-333.

41. Lake reports that new federal legislation now allows unions to bargain for day-care as a fringe benefit. Lake, *op. cit.*, p. 97.

42. *Ibid.*, p. 96.

Methods of Research and Interviewing

The study is based on a detailed analysis of twenty-seven couples. The main focus is on twenty "professional" couples in which the wife had an independent career of her own. There were also seven "traditional" couples in which the wife curtailed her career; these cases were used for comparison and mainly to make certain findings visible that otherwise would have been overlooked.

Rationale for the Sample Selection

The main aim in obtaining the sample was to select *strategic cases* for study; in other words, those cases which would reveal the most theoretically about the problem. For this reason, several possible approaches were eliminated. For example, it would have been possible to select a random sample representative of the U.S. population as a whole. Or it would have been possible to study a cohort, such as students of a certain school or class, and see what had happened to them since obtaining their professional education. Samples obtained through such approaches would have included a continuum of types of women. They would have included not only housewives and careerists, but also every conceivable variation between these extremes. This approach is valuable for certain questions.[1]

But in the present study it was thought that the opposite approach would be more useful because certain problems can be seen more clearly if the focus is mainly on one clear-cut group, rather than on a continuum. Thus the decision was made to focus on couples in which the wife did follow an independent career of her own. They are strategic in that they are one type and furthermore, in that they are highly atypical in the society as a whole. Most women do not have careers. For purposes of understanding, it is very often more useful to look at the atypical case because that is where certain features of the problem are highlighted and seen in a more prominent form.

This type of analysis which, for purposes of understanding, focuses on the atypical cases has a special name. Sociologists call it the *analysis of deviant cases.* The name is not meant to imply any kind of unfavorable judgment. Rather, it is a technical term referring to the study of cases which depart from the more typical pattern. This type of analysis owes much of its current respectability to Lazarsfeld's suggestion that deviant cases have a *positive* role in empirical research. Reviewing the method, Kendall and Wolf note that previously deviant cases were considered a source of embarrassment. Researchers used to try to explain away these loose ends and make their findings appear neater. Kendall and Wolf suggest that one function of deviant case analysis is to "uncover relevant *additional factors* which had not previously been considered."[2] Lipset, Trow, and Coleman also discuss this method in connection with their study of democracy in the International Typographic Union. If one already knows that a given behavior pattern — such as oligarchy in large unions — is common, then repeated study of the same pattern will not produce many new insights. However, a deviant case — for example, a more democratic union — suggests that the theoretical structure is oversimplified and that it requires the incorporation of additional variables.[3] Yet deviant case analysis actually is not as new as these investigators make it sound. Robert E. Park long ago recommended studying the atypical. He advocated, for example, the study of the marginal man, the cultural hybrid, because it is in his mind where conflicting cultures meet and fuse. "It is, therefore, in the mind of the marginal man that the process of civilization is visibly going on, and it is in the mind of the marginal man that the process of civilization may best be studied."[4]

A second aim of sampling was to have some comparative information. A kind of blindness can occur if a researcher looks at only one type of case. The study is not comparative in the strictest sense of the term, but some interviews were also done with couples in which the wife curtailed her career. These comparison cases are used primarily in order to make certain findings visible that otherwise would have been overlooked. In over half the comparison cases, for example, there was a very asymmetrical helping relationship. A major responsibility of the wife was to arrange her entire life so as to promote the husband's career. This extremely asymmetrical pattern never appeared in the two-career couples. But its absence would have been overlooked without the use of comparative data. A third aim, which will be discussed later, was to keep the sample small.

The present aim of selecting strategic cases for investigation has much in common with Glaser and Strauss' strategy of "theoretical sampling." In other words, the aim is not to represent the population at large, but rather to choose a sample on the basis of learning something about certain theoretical categories. Glaser and Strauss emphasize the importance of distinguishing between this type of sampling and statistical random sampling:

> Their differences should be kept clearly in mind for both designing research and judging its credibility. Theoretical sampling is done in order to discover categories and their properties, and to suggest the interrelationships into a theory. Statistical sampling is done to obtain accurate evidence on distributions of people among categories to be used in descriptions or verifications.[5]

It is important to remember the differences between these because that which constitutes an "adequate sample" is very different in the two kinds of research. They suggest that an adequate theoretical sample should be judged according to "how widely and diversely the analyst chose his groups for saturating categories according to the type of theory he wished to develop."[6] In contrast, the adequate statistical sample should be judged according to the techniques of random and stratified sampling which were used.

Locating Couples for the Study

Couples were obtained by selecting wives who met the criteria such as type of occupation and age which were discussed in Chapter Two. Because relatively few married women actually have professions, selecting wives was the most efficient way to obtain couples with two careers. Occupational and other information about the husband was not necessarily known ahead of time, but it was predicted that most of their husbands would also have professional or similar occupations. Other studies have suggested that this would be so. For example, a recent large survey showed that of married women with doctorates in sciences, social sciences, and humanities, respectively 89, 84, and 84 percent of their husbands had professional occupations. And if one considers both professional and proprietor/managerial husbands, then respectively 95, 95, and 92 percent of their husbands fell into this combined category.[7]

First of all, the more apparently systematic ways of obtaining names were investigated: for example, directories of professional associations, *American Men of Science*, college catalogues. The major drawbacks of these listings were that most were out-of-date (frequently data collected several years ago), or they did not give the necessary information (e.g., they did not give marital status, or one could not tell the person's sex because first names were omitted). In view of these many drawbacks, it was decided that sampling from such lists would have just as many biases as a more informal approach.

Thus, it was decided to obtain the cases through a variety of informal means. Including the preliminary cases, a total of twenty-nine couples was interviewed. Of these seven were obtained from professional directories or associations, two from college catalogues, two from newspaper articles, two were recommended by previous respondents, six by Brandeis University faculty members, four by Brandeis graduate students, and six by other professional people. Thus many cases were obtained through a modified network approach — but the researcher was the only common link in the chain. This approach avoided, for the most part, getting the people interviewed to refer me to their own friends and it also avoided getting numerous names from any one person. Otherwise, the people included in the study might have been linked together by some other characteristic they had in common such as membership in ethnic organizations or political groups.

The couples were approached first by telephoning the wife. Of thirty-two women telephoned, twenty-nine agreed to participate. All of these twenty-nine were interviewed. In the three cases where the women declined to participate, the stated reason for refusal was lack of time. This claim was then supported by a detailed description of their busy schedules. One woman also said that she was tired of answering questions about women's careers.

In each couple the wife was interviewed first and then the husband was also asked. In the twenty-nine couples, only three husbands declined to participate. Of these three, two husbands declined to participate at all. The third did talk rather openly a while on the telephone, but was adamant about refusing a longer personal interview on the grounds of time. Attitudinal information from these three husbands was thus either completely missing or limited. However, information on the career patterns of these men was available in biographical directories. The stated reasons for refusal in two cases were lack of time. This claim was then supported by detailed descriptions of their schedules. The third man said simply, "I never do that sort of thing."

In general, the main entree problem was lack of time. As discussed in the chapter on allocation of time and effort, most people interviewed were extremely busy. Even those most interested in the subject matter of the research sometimes found it difficult to arrange an appointment.

Data Collection
Data were gathered primarily by means of "free-style" interviews. In other words, the accent was on flexibility. An interview guide of general topics was used rather than a rigid questionnaire schedule. The interviews were "standardized" only in the sense that there was a

given list of topics to be discussed with each person. The interviews were primarily "nonschedule standardized," to use the terminology of the classification system of Richardson, Dohrenwend, and Klein, which differentiates between "schedule standardized," "nonschedule standardized," and "nonstandardized" interviews.

> Instead of using a schedule of questions, the nonschedule standardized interviewer works with a list of the information required from each respondent. . . . For each respondent, the interviewer formulates questions to get at the same meaning. . . . The schedule standardized interviewer asks the *same question* of each respondent and hopes this will have the same meaning, whereas the nonschedule interviewer formulates the *classes of information* he is seeking and hopes he can formulate the questions in such a way that they will have the same meaning for each respondent.[8]

The wording of questions and the sequence of topics varied from person to person. In many instances, people themselves spontaneously brought up topics which were on the list, e.g., domestic help, competitiveness, spouse's attitude. Whenever this occurred, these topics were then followed up as "naturally" as possible; in other words, in a manner approximating that of a conversation. Much of the interviewing consisted of listening, and then asking further specific probes only after the person had covered a topic in his own way.

These procedures are in keeping with the assumptions which underlie nonschedule standardized interviews and which include the following ideas. 1) If the meaning of questions is to be standardized, then one must be free to adapt the wording. 2) There is no fixed sequence of questions which will be satisfactory to all respondents; the most effective sequence is one determined by the respondent's readiness and willingness to take up topics. These assumptions are contrary, of course, to those underlying schedule standardized interviews where it is believed that the stimulus for each respondent must be identical; that to be an identical stimulus, the question must be worded identically each time it is presented; and that since all previous parts of the interview are part of the stimulus context, the sequence of questions must be identical. As Richardson, Dohrenwend, and Klein note, both the schedule and nonschedule approaches to standardizing interviews rest on assumptions that are largely untested.[9]

Other portions of the interview collected 1) nonstandardized information and 2) schedule standardized data. First of all, completely nonstandardized information was gathered from any respondent as long as the material seemed relevant to the overall study. For example, in one case, it turned out that a husband had recently been in the position of hiring a man whose career decisions were complicated by the profession of the man's wife. With this husband, the issue of a husband and wife getting jobs was discussed not only from the point of view of his own private life as a job applicant, but also from his vantage point as an employer of other such couples. Here this person had idiosyncratic information that was relevant to the overall study, but no attempt was made to get similar information from all couples. In other cases originally nonstandardized topics were then added to the interview guide. For example, in an early interview a woman spontaneously mentioned her opinion of day-time child-care centers. It was believed that this would be a good topic to discuss with all respondents and so subsequently each person was asked about it. Secondly, at the end of the interview some schedule standardized demographic data were obtained on a one-page questionnaire; for example, information like year of birth and year of birth of each child.

The very flexible interviewing approach was chosen originally as a strategy to get people to remember more easily and to talk more freely; some had had difficulty with a few early interviews that were more rigid in style. But the flexibility had other advantages too. First of all, as has already been mentioned, it allowed for uncovering new ideas and topics in the course of the study. These new ideas were handled in either one of two ways. When new ideas were uncovered early in the interviewing stage, data on the topic could be gathered from all, or almost all, respondents; the only difference was that in the early interviews the information appeared spontaneously and in the later ones it was asked systematically. When new ideas were uncovered late in the interviewing stage, data could only be obtained on them from less than the total sample. In the report, these ideas are discussed as suggestive leads for future research. It is stated explicitly that they are not based on data from the entire sample.

A second analytical benefit of flexible interviewing is that one can then observe the links that people spontaneously make between various topics. These links can be interesting findings in themselves. For example, professional women often brought up the issue of the importance of the husband's attitude spontaneously, often returned to it, and stressed it as essential. They linked the importance of the husband's attitude to other issues such as how they were able to get both career and home responsibilities done or how the husband overlooked certain inconveniences due to the wife's career. In contrast, the traditional wives did not make similar links and did not see the husband's attitude as such a crucial issue.

The flexibility in interviewing had its practical advantages too. It was sometimes hard to isolate the person for the entire interview; a child, spouse, employee, or friend might wander in. The changeable order of the questions made it possible to postpone topics which would have been embarrassing to discuss in front of such other people.

Two other features about the style of interviewing are relevant for understanding the analysis. First of all, for many topics, information was gathered in response to direct questions on a topic and also indirectly wherever it happened to come up in the conversation. In the analysis, account was taken of both sources of data.

Secondly, throughout the interview an attempt was made to get people to support any general answer with concrete details. Thus if people said that the child-care help had been satisfactory (or not satisfactory) they were asked to specify the criteria by which they made this judgment; e.g., the help was reliable or unreliable in terms of coming to work, the help made the child independent or dependent, etc. And if they said, for example, that the hired help made the child more dependent, then they were asked to describe concretely an instance where they thought this had occurred. Also if they said that something happened a lot or seldom, or that a problem was serious or trivial, they were asked to specify what *they* meant by these adjectives. The emphasis on concrete detail helped diminish misunderstanding of what they were saying; made explicit what dimensions of a topic concerned them (e.g., what aspects of child care were the important ones); and made it possible for the researcher to make an independent judgment (e.g., a woman might say her husband helped her a lot more than other professional women's husbands; with the concrete description of his help, the researcher could make an independent judgment of how this case compared to others in the study).

A major problem in carrying out the study was arranging times for the interviews. Almost all of the people interviewed had very hectic and tight schedules. To find an hour or two for talk was sometimes very difficult. In some cases, appointments were made several weeks in advance. The time (weekday, weekend, or evening) and the place (home or office) were at the convenience of the respondent. Interviews with the wives averaged 2¼ hours (range: 1 to 4 hours), and those with the husband averaged 1½ hours (range: ½ hour to 3 hours).

The fact that both spouses were interviewed increased the length of the data-gathering period. Contacting and interviewing twenty-nine couples required more time than fifty-eight unrelated individuals would have taken — primarily because the husband was never contacted until after the wife's interview. (This order was adopted partly for strategic reasons: it was believed that the wives would be initially more interested in the subject matter and more willing to participate. In some cases the order was also a practical necessity since the identity of the husband was not known before the wife's interview.)

The interviews with the husbands were believed to be particularly important since one of the predictions of the study was that the husband's attitude would be of major importance in determining whether the wife pursued or curtailed her career. Interviewing both husband and wife was a departure from a common practice of relying solely on the wife/mother's report of a situation. Making the couple the unit of analysis was another departure from common practice. Investigators interested in women's careers have typically taken the woman as the focus of the study, and have talked of how her career is influenced by her husband. This is, of course, important. But it seemed important also to investigate whether the opposite occurred — whether her career influenced his. And to get this information, it seemed especially important to interview the husbands themselves.

Information in the first few interviews was recorded by taking notes. But it was difficult to capture all the subtle nuances of the conversation in this manner. Therefore it was decided to try tape-recording. Of forty-four people asked about tape-recording, thirty-eight agreed immediately. Three were a bit hesitant at first, but did not seem uncomfortable once the tape-recorder was started. Only three people requested that I take notes instead. Of course, many of the people were accustomed to speaking before microphones and to using dictating machines and tape-recorders in their own work. Some had their own tape-recorders which they used for practicing lectures or for interviewing other people.

The empirical data of the study consisted mainly of the free-style interviews just described. These data were supplemented by information from a variety of other sources; for example, career information from directories like *Who's Who* and *American Men of Science*, and a certain amount of observational data one gets in connection with an interview ("life-style" observations on home furnishing, dress; interaction of the person with spouse or children; nonverbal responses including tone of voice, nervous mannerisms, etc.). In some cases information was also obtained by reading book reviews of the person's published works, newspaper articles about them, and reading articles that they themselves had written. This supplementary information proved useful in a variety of ways.

Observational data were used to confirm (or to question) what the person said in the interview. For example, one woman said that her husband helped a lot with the children; and indeed, while I was interviewing her, the husband was looking after the children and playing with them. In another case, the woman said her husband helped share the car-pool driving; and indeed while I was at their home he just returned from having driven the children home from school that day. Also in some cases observational data helped clarify what the person was saying. One woman's desk was almost geometrically neat and orderly — with only one or two letters scattered on it. But she claimed her desk was messy, and it bothered her that it was this way. This gave a clue as to how high her standards of neatness were and why it took a lot of energy on her part to combine work and domestic tasks.

The biographical directory information was very useful in that it provided exact years people were at various places and gave formal job titles. Directories could not be used for selecting the sample for reasons already discussed, but they could be used for information on prior positions. It is difficult for people to switch back and forth between an objective level of questioning (e.g., date a job was held) and subjective levels of questioning (e.g., how they felt about changing jobs). By relying on directories for dates as much as possible, the interview could be focused more on the latter type of information.

Justification for the Small-Sample Approach

Because the dominant trend in social science research is toward more quantitative work, perhaps special attention should be devoted to justifying the use of the small-sample approach. The reasons for what types of cases were selected for the sample have already been discussed. What we are talking about here is the size of the sample.

One important justification for doing a small-sample study is that it can *complement* existing survey studies. For example, large-scale quantitative data exist already on such topics as female participation in the labor force. The present study is thus complementary — it is an attempt to see the story behind certain quantitative trends.

It also was decided that dense, "free-style" interviews would also help prevent the drawing of over-hasty conclusions concerning the direction of "cause-effect" in certain correlations which have been shown between work and family. For example, it is true that family contingencies will affect a person's work, and it is true that there is an inverse correlation between the number of children an educated woman has and the number of years she is in the labor force. This does not necessarily mean that the number of children a woman has determines the course of her work career. The cause-effect direction may well be the other way around — her work career may determine the number of children she has. It is this type of information — the story behind the numerical correlations — which can be explored in a small-sample study.

Furthermore, there are two particularly persuasive arguments in the literature which can be used in support of a small-sample study — one by Weiss and one by Roth. Weiss is concerned with alternative ways to study complex situations — situations in which as many of the inter-related phenomena as possible are studied simultaneously. The re-searcher, after appreciating the multifarious phenomena of such a situation, must search for some simplification in order to understand it. The simplification of such complexity, Weiss suggests, may proceed in either of two directions. These approaches he calls the analytic and the holistic. A researcher using the analytic approach would see his task as isolating the elements from each other and identifying a small number of relationships. He might, for example, focus on particular independent-dependent relationships. In contrast, the researcher using the holistic approach will try to identify the nature of the system and will look for a whole system of interrelated elements. The question he asks is, "Taking it all together, how does the whole thing work?"[10] Weiss makes the following comparison:

> What goes on in the mind of an investigator who, whenever he is asked to study a complex situation, thinks of survey research? He probably as-sumes that the task of research is to discover consistent relationships between elements, that consistency can be demonstrated only within a large sample, that relationships can be established and evaluated only with reliable measures. The result is a survey. A holistic assumption, on the other hand, that the aim of research is to discover the organization of elements, would lead to different emphases and consequently to different research designs.[11]

Indeed, holistic assessment requires collecting data on a great range of issues. "Only in this way can the investigator be assured that the data have within them a report of the functioning of each of the sys-tem's elements. This . . . leads to the case study or small sample study as preferred research designs."[12] One reason it would be hard to do holistic assessment through survey research is that the investigator would have to have a very good understanding of the system *before* he began to write the survey schedule. And if one already understands the system so well, the question then arises as to whether it is worthwhile to then do an expensive survey.

In doing holistic research, the aim is not to test a set of hypotheses; rather, the aim is to discover organization, patterning, or system in that which is being studied. Perhaps for this reason, holistic research frequently is labeled exploratory, hypothesis-generating, and preliminary to a more hypothesis-testing approach. Weiss, however, maintains that in actual practice this rarely turns out to be so. In actuality either approach may support the other.

If one does not necessarily expect holistic research to be followed by more "definitive research," then it becomes especially important to raise the issue of generalizability. Weiss asks whether findings of holistic research can be generalized when they are based on only one or a few cases. Obviously, there is no appropriate statistical argument. Yet in actual practice holistic research is used as a basis for generalization.[13] Weiss suggests two possible arguments.

> One argument for generalizing from a single case is that the system discovered is a necessary consequence of the environmental pressures under which the case functions. . . .
> Another, somewhat different, argument for generalizing is that the essential characteristics of the situation itself require a particular system. Here it is not the surround of the unit under study, but the unit itself, its aims and character, which establishes a certain system.[14]

Much of the present report focuses on what has happened to those specific people included in the study — with no claim to hypothesis-testing, frequency distribution in the population, etc. But, insofar as it was deemed desirable to generalize from this small sample, it has been done on the basis of Weiss' first argument; namely, that the organization of these couples' lives is a consequence of environmental pressures — specifically those pressures resulting from the occupational and familial arrangements prevalent in the middle class and upper-middle class in the contemporary United States.

Roth also presents a very persuasive argument which can be used in support of a small-sample study. Writing along a very different line of thought, his justification for samples of moderate size is in terms of avoiding hired-hand research and its associated dangers. Roth likens hired-hand research workers to the hired hand (e.g., machine shop operator) in a production organization. So far, research on "restriction of production" and deviation from assigned duties has been done primarily on factory workers and other such low-prestige groups. But there is no reason to believe a hired hand in scientific research will behave any differently from other hired hands. Why should the flunky, who is hired to do somebody else's dirty work, bother to be careful or accurate or precise. Roth discusses the effect of hired-hand mentality on the product, and then states:

> More important, however, I believe the need for hired hands has been greatly exaggerated. Why, for example, must we so often have large

samples? The large sample is frequently a contrivance for controlling various kinds of "errors" (including the "error" introduced by unreliable hired hands). But if the study were done on a much smaller sample by one person or several colleagues who formulated their own study and conducted it entirely by themselves, much of this error would not enter in the first place. Isn't a sample of fifty which yields data in which we can have a high degree of confidence more useful than a sample of five thousand where we must remain doubtful about what it is that we have collected?[15]

Roth recognizes that hired-hand mentality can occur in research staffs of any size — even where a professor hires an individual student to do his research chores. However, he states that when there are only a small number of researchers working together there is a better opportunity of developing true colleagueship. The larger the group, the more difficult it is for each person to formulate and carry out some of his own ideas.

NOTES

1. The cohort approach has been used in several studies of women's careers. See, for example, Eli Ginzberg with Associates, *Life Styles of Educated Women* (New York: Columbia University, 1966). The cohort approach, incidentally, usually involves data collected through mailed questionnaires since by the time the study is conducted, the people are scattered around the world.

2. Patricia L. Kendall and Katherine M. Wolf, "The Analysis of Deviant Cases in Communications Research," *Communications Research 1948-49*, eds. Paul F. Lazarsfeld and Frank N. Stanton (New York: Harper, 1949), p. 153.

3. Seymour Martin Lipset, Martin A. Trow, and James S. Coleman, *Union Democracy* (Garden City, New York: Doubleday Anchor Books, 1962), p. 469. (First published in 1956: The Free Press.)

4. Robert E. Park, "Human Migration and the Marginal Man," *American Journal of Sociology*, 33 (May, 1928), p. 881.

5. Barney G. Glaser and Anselm L. Strauss, *The Discovery of Grounded Theory: Strategies for Qualitative Research* (Chicago: Aldine Publishing Co., 1967), p. 62.

6. *Ibid.*, p. 63.

7. Rita James Simon, Shirley Merritt Clark, and Kathleen Galway, "The Woman Ph.D.: A Recent Profile," *Social Problems*, 15 (Fall, 1967), p. 223.

8. Stephen A. Richardson, Barbara Snell Dohrenwend, and David Klein, *Interviewing: Its Forms and Functions* (New York: Basic Books, 1965), p. 45.

9. *Ibid.*, p. 51.

10. Robert S. Weiss, "Alternative Approaches In The Study Of Complex Situations," *Human Organization*, 25 (Fall, 1966), p. 199.

11. *Ibid.*, p. 201.

12. Robert S. Weiss, "Issues In Holistic Research," *Institutions And The Person: Papers Presented To Everett C. Hughes*, eds. Howard S. Becker *et al.* (Chicago: Aldine, 1968), p. 345

13. Zola has suggested one reason *why* people generalize from holistic research. (This is, of course, a separate issue from whether or not they are scientifically justified in doing so.) He suggests that it is "politically" easier to generalize from holistic than from survey research. With the former, one can more easily get the policy or political point across. The latter gets too bogged down with qualifications, probabilities, and percentages. As such, it loses impact. Irving Kenneth Zola, private communication.

14. Weiss, "Issues In Holistic Research," p. 350.

15. Julius A. Roth, "Hired Hand Research," *The American Sociologist*, 1 (August, 1966), p. 195.

Professional and Traditional Couples: Descriptive Data

Though the aim of the study was to find out about the problems facing the two-career family in general, this was done, of course, by looking at the experiences of specific people. Thus it might be worthwhile to present a brief profile of the social and economic characteristics of those persons who were included in the study. As has been stated before, only five characteristics were known prior to the interviews; namely, the wife's occupation, marital status, wife's age, where the couple lived, and whether the wife had pursued her career. These characteristics were used to select the sample. In contrast, the characteristics discussed in this Appendix were not used in selecting the sample, but rather are pieces of information obtained during the course of the interviews.

Ethnic Background
Slightly over half of the parents of the people interviewed were foreign born. Almost all of these foreign-born parents were European, with Europe broadly defined to include the British Isles, western and eastern European countries, and the western U.S.S.R. There were no differences between the professional group and the traditional group in the percentage of foreign-born parents. There was no difference in percentage of foreign born between the categories of wife's mother, wife's father, husband's mother, and husband's father.

All of the people interviewed were Caucasian. Over a third were foreign born. There was no difference in percentage foreign born between the professional and traditional groups; and there was no difference in percentage foreign born between males and females.

Most of the people interviewed who were born in the United States were born in northeastern states. However, only six were born in Massachusetts itself. A few were from the South and a few from the Middle West (e.g., Illinois, Indiana). None were from any state west of the Mississippi River.

Among the parents, ethnic intermarriage was not very common. Of the fifty-two parental couples where complete ethnic information was obtained, only eight intermarried across ethnic lines (ethnicity defined by country of birth).[1] In comparison to their parents, the people interviewed had a much higher incidence of ethnic intermarriage. Defining ethnicity as country of birth, one third of the present marriages among the respondents were ethnically mixed. And if one assigns people to ethnic categories based on parents' origin — in keeping with the assumption that certain cultural traditions continue even after immigration — the figure is even higher. Using this definition of ethnicity, half of the respondents had ethnic intermarriages.

Religious Background

The people in the study came primarily from Protestant and Jewish families. A few came from Catholic families or families with no religion. This same distribution occurred in all four groups — both men and women, and both the professional and traditional groups. In comparing these four groups, the only noticeable difference was the greater tendency of professional wives to minimize the role that religion played in their parents' lives. Eight of the twenty professional wives came from families which either had no religion or from families which were "not very religious" or "not practicing."

Among the parents of the people interviewed, there was a striking absence of religious intermarriage. Complete religious information was obtained for forty-nine parental couples. In only one of these forty-nine couples did the marriage cross the categories of Protestant, Catholic, Jewish, Other, None. There were, however, some cases of intermarriage between various types of Protestants. In contrast, in the respondents' own generation one third of the couples had religious intermarriages; that is, the present marriage crossed over the categories of Protestant, Catholic, Jewish, Other, None. (Seven of the twenty professional couples and two of the seven traditional couples intermarried.)

Among the people interviewed, the number of couples who intermarried religiously and/or ethnically was even higher; some marriages were religiously but not ethnically mixed, and vice versa. Seventeen of the twenty-seven couples had religious and/or ethnic intermarriages.[2]

Educational Level of the Parents

The respondents' parents had very diverse educational backgrounds; there was little difference between male and female or between the professional and traditional groups in this respect. This diversity of educational background among the parental generation is shown in Table 1.

TABLE 1

Educational Level of Parental Generation for All Respondents*

0 - 8th grade	22
Begin high school to end high school	28
Begin college to graduate college	33
Beyond college	14
Unknown	11
	108

*Such broad educational categories were used for two reasons. First of all, respondents did not always know the exact educational level of the parents; a respondent might know that a parent had had some high school education but be unable to supply information on the exact grade. Secondly, the parents came from a great variety of educational systems which are hard to translate precisely into American school grades; e.g., a European apprentice system, private tutoring.

Work History and Occupational Level of the Couples' Parents

The Wife's Parents. In the professional group, almost half of the wives' mothers had extensive work histories, that is, worked not only before but also after marriage and motherhood. By contrast, in the traditional group none of the wives' mothers had extensive work histories. In other words, if the wife's mother had an extensive work history, the wife did too. This information is shown in Table 2. Only in the professional group does one find any wives' mothers who worked after marriage and after children. In the traditional group only three of the seven mothers ever worked, and none worked after marriage.

As regards type of work done by the wives' mothers, they had primarily middle-class occupations. In the professional group, of those wives' mothers who worked at some time, most (14 out of 17) had middle-class jobs. Of these, however, only two held jobs requiring education beyond the college level (e.g., physician, professor). In the traditional group so few wives' mothers ever worked that one cannot make a general statement about their type of occupation.

The wives' fathers in both groups had primarily middle-class or upper-middle-class occupations. A large number of different specific occupations were represented.

TABLE 2

Work History of the Wife's Mother and Career History of Wife

Work History of the Wife's Mother	Occupational Situation of Wife	
	Professional Group	Traditional Group
Never Worked — neither before marriage, during marriage, or later as a widow.	3	4
Worked only before marriage (or before children); never returned to work again.	6	3
Worked before marriage (or children); unemployed all through child-rearing; returned to work or school only very late in life (e.g., at age 50 or 60).	2	0
Worked before marriage; worked after marriage in a way that merged with family responsibilities; e.g., help manage family business or contract to sew within the home.*	3	0
Worked through majority of adult years — before marriage, after marriage, and through much of child-rearing period.	6	0
	20	7

*One woman who worked only after marriage was counted in this category. As always, women combine work and domestic responsibilities in so many different ways that it is difficult to place them in categories.

The Husband's Parents. The findings regarding work history and occupational level of husbands' parents are very similar to those regarding wives' parents. First of all, husbands' mothers were more likely to have been employed in the professional group than in the traditional group. In the professional group a little over a third of the husbands' mothers had extensive work histories. In the traditional group only one of the husbands' mothers had an extensive work history, and for most of her life this was as a farmer's wife rather than employment away from the home. The work history of the husbands' mothers is shown in Table 3.

TABLE 3
Work History of Husband's Mother and Career History of Wife

Work History of the Husband's Mother*	Occupational Situation of Wife	
	Professional Group	Traditional Group
Never worked — neither before marriage, during marriage, or later as a widow.	3	1
Worked only before marriage (or before children); never returned to work again.	6	4
Worked before marriage (or children); unemployed all through child-rearing; returned to work or school only very late in life (e.g., at age 50 or 60).	1	1
Worked before marriage; worked after marriage in a way that merged with family responsibilities; e.g., help manage family business or contract to sew within the home.	4	1**
Worked through majority of adult years — before marriage, after marriage, and through much of child-rearing period.	2 / 16	0 / 7

*There were also four professional group cases which did not fit these categories: two mothers did minor amount of sporadic work after marriage, 1 mother worked extensively after divorce out of economic necessity, and 1 was unknown.
**This was a farmer's wife.

These trends regarding work history of the husbands' mother are in the same direction as those for the wife's mother. Looking at only the professional group, the percentage of wives' mothers with extensive work histories is so similar to the percentage of husbands' mothers, that one wonders if the extensive maternal work histories occurred in the same couples. Actually, the overlap was small (three); thus, in thirteen of the twenty professional couples the wife's mother or the husband's mother or both had an extensive work history. This suggests that having a model of a working mother — no matter which side of the family it is on — leads to the wife herself having a career.

As regards type of work done by husbands' mothers, most who worked had middle-class occupations. In the professional group, of those husbands' mothers who worked, ten out of fifteen had middle-class occupations. Of these, however, only one held a job that required education beyond the college level; she was a physician. The husbands' fathers in both groups had primarily middle-class or upper-middle-class occupations.

A Brief Profile of the Couples

Work. The professional wives worked in universities, hospitals, industry, or research labs. Academic jobs were the most common in this group. Fourteen of the twenty had academic jobs when interviewed. Their ranks ranged from lecturer or assistant professor up to full professor. The most frequent rank was associate professor, with seven at this level. The others worked in industry, hospitals, or research institutes, holding either research positions or doing administrative work.

It was expected that these highly educated women would marry highly educated men, and indeed both the professional and traditional women did. Almost all the men held an advanced degree comparable to that of their wives — a dental, medical, or doctoral degree. The few exceptions were business men.

Husbands in the professional couples interviewed held a variety of positions, but thirteen of these twenty men were in academic positions. Their ranks were associate professor or higher. The most common rank was full professor; nine were at this level. Other husbands held exclusively research positions, did administrative work, or had business careers. Among the traditional couples, the husbands held a variety of positions.

In most (two thirds) of the professional couples, the husband and wife were in different fields; in the remaining third, the spouses were in the same field. In almost all the traditional couples, the spouses were in different fields.

Family. Most couples in both groups had been married to each other for ten to twenty years when interviewed. It was not necessarily their first marriage. Among the women, four of the twenty professional wives and three of the seven traditional wives had been divorced and re-married. Among the men, five in the professional group, but none in the traditional group had been previously married. The remarriages were second marriages, with the sole exception of one man who had been married several times.

Most professional and all traditional women were first married when they were in their twenties. The few late first marriages — that is, where the bride was thirty years or older — were all in the professional group. As to age of wife at time of present marriage, when late marriages occurred they were again in the professional group. Most professional wives and all traditional wives had their first child when they were in their twenties. When instances of late motherhood occurred, they were in the professional group.

Income. The people interviewed, in general, fell into relatively high income brackets compared to the population as a whole. Most couples in both groups had family incomes of over $20,000 a year.[3] Slightly over a third of the professional couples had a family income of $30,000 or higher. However, in the traditional group, a family income of over $30,000 was rare.

Slightly over half of the professional wives themselves made between $10,000 and $20,000 a year. In almost all cases, the husband made more money than the wife. But certainly in the professional group, most of the wives contributed a substantial share of the family income. And, in a few cases, the wife's earned income was more than the husband's by several thousand dollars.

NOTES

1. Obviously, more precise ethnic categories would be required if ethnicity was a major focus of the study, or if one was concerned with rates of intermarriage within a large multi-ethnic society like the United States where so many ethnic groups all have the same country of birth.

2. Based on the higher of the two figures of ethnic intermarriage previously presented.

3. This figure means total family income, before taxes, from all sources — salaries of husband and of wife; other earned income such as consulting fees, lecture fees; and income from investments.

1 2 3 4 5 6 7 8 9–RRD–79 78 77 76 75 74 73 72